OUT AT HOME

OUT AT HOME

The True Story of Glenn Burke,
Baseball's First Openly Gay Player

GLENN BURKE

with Erik Sherman

BERKLEY BOOKS, NEW YORK

THE BERKLEY PUBLISHING GROUP
Published by the Penguin Group
Penguin Group (USA) LLC
375 Hudson Street, New York, New York 10014

USA • Canada • UK • Ireland • Australia • New Zealand • India • South Africa • China

penguin.com

A Penguin Random House Company

OUT AT HOME

BERKLEY® is a registered trademark of Penguin Group (USA) LLC.
The "B" design is a trademark of Penguin Group (USA) LLC.

Berkley trade paperback ISBN: 978-0-425-28143-7

An application to register this book for cataloging has been submitted to the Library of Congress.

PUBLISHING HISTORY
Excel Publishing trade paperback edition / 1995
Berkley trade paperback edition / March 2015

Cover design by Jason Gill

147204767

To all my loving family and friends
—Glenn Burke

To Virginia Hunt for giving a kid a chance;
Mom, Dad, and JC for their encouragement;
Lutha Burke for her love and kindness;
and Tim Neverett, and Jim Cerny
for their input and enthusiasm toward this project
—Erik Sherman

CONTENTS

FOREWORD BY BILLY BEAN, MAJOR LEAGUE BASEBALL AMBASSADOR FOR INCLUSION

As a player, I remember hearing Glenn Burke's name from time to time. There were brief stories about a gay ballplayer who played for the Los Angeles Dodgers in the seventies, but I always left that subject alone as I was navigating a life of my own deep inside the closet. I certainly had wondered about him, especially after hearing rumors of him living on the street, ill, and struggling with drug addiction, but I chose to ignore them. I knew that was only one side of the story, and the familiar stereotypical tone made me angry. Ironically, while playing Winter Baseball in Venezuela in the late eighties, a few of the guys were listening to some stories from one of my teammates, a lefty pitcher named Steve Shirley. He came up through the Dodgers organization, and on this long bus trip, he was describing some of the great players that he'd played with in the minor leagues. He said the two best minor league players he ever saw were Pedro Guerrero and "a guy" named Glenn Burke. There was no talk of Glenn being gay, just that he was a stud who could have played any sport and been a star. Glenn was getting some serious respect from a veteran who had played a long time and knew the game well.

I hadn't thought about Glenn much until I saw an incredibly well-produced story done by Keith Olbermann on ESPN in 1995. Glenn was dying of AIDS, and Keith captured the sadness of a career and life that were derailed by homophobia, discrimination, betrayal, addiction, and ultimately AIDS. The story was like a knife to my heart. I had just experienced the death of my own partner, Sam, weeks before, and seeing images of Glenn on TV, emaciated and fighting death with each breath, was too much. A wave of grief and sadness came over me and the tears wouldn't stop.

In 2003, when the circumstances of my own life led me to writing my book, *Going the Other Way: Lessons from a Life In and Out of Major League Baseball*, I remembered that moment, and even though I didn't know his entire story, I dedicated my book to Glenn. It was my own way of honoring his courage as a major league baseball player, who just happened to be gay. We never met, but we were brothers, and we always will be. We all know that in the entire 145-year history of major league baseball, he and I *could not* be the only two gay men who have played in the big leagues, yet we are the only ones recognized to have done so.

Glenn was much braver than I. He refused to let homophobia change him. He didn't hide from his truth. (I struggled heavily with my sexuality, and I never came out until I had left baseball for good, and it's a choice I'll always regret). Glenn had his loving family, and a hometown group of friends around him for support. He was so far ahead of his time, brimming with self-confidence, yet naive enough to believe the rest of the world would be accepting, just like his family. He learned quickly that a few powerful people in baseball decided his fate. They sent their message loud and clear, which led to his decision to stop playing.

This book was not easy for me, yet I read it in one sitting, spellbound. It brought back memories of my darkest times. Erik Sherman writes a gut-wrenching, and incredibly honest account of the world through Glenn's own words. At times Glenn seemed to be his own worst enemy, and his loyalty to some, especially the most personal, led to his downfall. I remember all too well the desire to trust others with my secret, but I was never able to share it. It's lonely in the closet, and the isolation tore me apart.

Our stories are different, but we both made a similar mistake. We didn't realize how much we loved our sport until we quit. Walking away from the game without reaching out for help was not the answer to our struggles. Adjusting to life after baseball is hard for every player, and Glenn's slide into darkness after his career ended breaks my heart. His life could have easily gone the other way. When I met Glenn's wonderful sister, Lutha Davis, at this year's 2014 MLB All-Star Game in Minnesota, I could still see the pain of Glenn's memory in her eyes. I'm certain that every image of baseball reminds her of her little brother, when he was young, healthy, strong, and a star in the making. His being recognized by MLB must have been bittersweet, but Lutha, and her daughter, Alice, were there, proudly representing their family. They shared some wonderful stories about Glenn with me, and I hate that I never got to meet him. His story will help change the sports world . . . for the better.

I was away from baseball for a very long time, but in my heart, I never left. As MLB's first Ambassador for Inclusion there is so much work to do. It is also my responsibility to represent the people in our sport who still play this game or work in secret, fearful of judgment as they work so hard to realize their dreams. I will champion Glenn's story, his highs and lows, and everything in between. He is back in baseball too, and I will help make sure that his memory is never forgotten.

INTRODUCTION

Baseball and Society

Nearly fifty years ago, a black athlete out of Cairo, Georgia, named Jackie Roosevelt Robinson broke the color barrier by becoming the first Negro to play major-league baseball. That was in April of 1947. Robinson's team, the Brooklyn Dodgers, instantly became synonymous with all that was right and fair with the world: three strikes you're out, three outs per inning, and if you're a human being with the tools to play in the big leagues, you can play baseball.

Many historians today consider Jackie Robinson to have been perhaps the greatest soldier in the struggle for black equality in this country. Not only did Robinson survive the death threats, racial slurs, and varying degrees of isolation, he also thrived on the ball field. During ten glorious seasons with a Dodger team that he led to six pennants and a memorable World Series championship over the hated Yankees, Robinson hit .311 en route to his induction into the Baseball Hall of Fame in 1962.

Nearly thirty years after Robinson broke baseball's color barrier, another black Dodger rookie, this one out of Oakland, California, came to understand another prejudice. This prejudice had nothing to do with the color of his skin. It was, instead, about his sexual preference. However, unlike Robinson's tumultuous first season, in his first Glenn Lawrence Burke, at six-two, 210 pounds, with movie star looks, was billed by scouts and coaches alike as "the next Willie Mays." Burke, however, was keeping his homosexuality a secret. Baseball was not ready to acknowledge gay people.

Glenn Burke and Baseball

Burke remained in the closet primarily because of his love of baseball. Ever since he put on his first baseball jersey in Little League, the game had been his whole life. Through the years he came to realize, like us all, that baseball is a macho sport and homophobia runs rampant through every locker room from coast to coast. With the exception of family and some close friends from a predominately gay section of San Francisco called the Castro, no one suspected Burke was a homosexual. His secret was safe from the baseball world. Safe, that is, for perhaps all of two seasons.

Two seasons, including a World Series appearance, had come and gone when it became obvious his secret was out. Dodger general manager Al Campanis, who years later would be fired from the ball club for racial remarks made on ABC's *Nightline*, pressured Burke to get married. Dodger manager Tommy Lasorda, who had an openly gay son who has since died of AIDS-related symptoms, resented Burke's friendship with Tom Jr., better known as Spunky. Lasorda, incidentally, is still said to be in denial about his son's death, claiming the cause of death to be ordinary pneumonia. So when Burke refused to get married or cool down his friendship with Spunky, he was soon traded to the Oakland A's for an aging Billy North. What everyone had begun to suspect about Burke was confirmed. Something was desperately wrong in Dodgertown when this business-savvy organization traded away a potential superstar for a player past his prime.

During an uninspired 1979 campaign with an A's team that had gone from being baseball's darlings in the early seventies to losing 108 games that season, Burke retired from baseball. However, he reconsidered the next spring and reported back to the A's. With new manager Billy Martin at the helm, there was a sense of excitement back in Oakland. However, when Martin began referring to Burke as a "faggot" on several occasions with some of the other players, the outfielder never had a chance. The prejudice, coupled with an injured knee, pushed Burke's hand to retire for good. Burke had been blackballed from baseball.

This isn't a story about judging how another chooses to live his life. It's rather a story of hypocrisy and how baseball went from being ahead of its time in changing America's social conscience to being a game that is clearly behind the times and has a set of standards that discourages participation by those who aren't heterosexual. From Babe Ruth to Steve Garvey, legend is made of their conquests. For the Glenn Burkes of the world, though, the coming out of their own sexual orientation is baseball suicide.

Burke has perhaps never completely gotten over being blackballed from the game he loves or the potential of what could have been a marvelous career cut short by prejudice. After falling victim to a car accident, heightened drug use, six months in a California penitentiary, and time on the streets, Burke now lives with his older sister in Oakland. He can barely walk and weighs a mere 135 pounds.

Glenn Burke is dying of AIDS.

WHY THE
BASEBALL ESTABLISHMENT
AND I NEVER SAW
EYE TO EYE

The pain is overwhelming. It hurts so much. The AIDS virus has given me incredible pain in my legs, which now have black lesions from my shins down to my toes. I am both warm and cold, hence the portable heater and air conditioner on a table next to my bed. Not long ago, I was 220 pounds of muscle. Now, I am a 130-pound man incapable of getting out of bed. I wear a diaper because I can no longer control my bodily functions. I need my loving sister Lutha and a full-time nurse to help me with things I used to take for granted. I can only speak in a whisper most of the time, so I can conserve my energy. On occasion, I cry uncontrollably from the mental and physical pain that is full-blown AIDS.

Little did anyone know on the evening of May 16, 1978, why I was really traded by the Los Angeles Dodgers to the Oakland

A's. After all, the man the Dodgers would receive in exchange was Billy North, a player who had watched his batting average drop sixty-four points in the previous two years. North was, of course, a switch-hitter, and that was a valuable asset to have in the big leagues. I, on the other hand, was only twenty-five years old, had started in two World Series' games for the Dodgers in '77, and had proven to the team and fans alike that I was a speed demon on the base paths and one of the better defensive outfielders in baseball. And if given the chance to play on a regular basis, I would have been a great hitter too. Many of the Dodger players were very upset by the trade. Steve Garvey and I cried. Don Sutton too. Dusty Baker and Davey Lopes were just pissed off. In fact, the two of them marched up to Dodger vice president Al Campanis's office and screamed, "You fuckin' assholes! You traded our best prospect. Not to mention the life of this team."

My secret of being homosexual was out. The Dodgers now knew I was gay. In the seventies, the Dodgers were drawing three million fans a year. They had a pristine, clean image. Management was afraid of my sexual orientation, even though I never flaunted it. To this day, the Dodgers deny trading me because I was gay. But it was painfully obvious.

Dodger manager Tommy Lasorda called me into his office after we had defeated the Pirates that night at Dodger Stadium. He told me, "We're tired of you walking back and forth in the dugout like a mad tiger in a cage. We're sending you to Oakland, where you can play more."

I could tell he was very uneasy about the trade. He knew he was trading away a top prospect for reasons having nothing to do with my abilities.

I probably should have seen the trade coming. Lasorda knew I was tight with his gay son Spunky. More on that later. And Campanis had offered me a bonus to find a woman and get married! Can you imagine that? Al said, "Everybody on this team is married but you, Glenn. When players get married on the Dodgers, we help them out financially. We can help you so you can go out and have a real nice honeymoon."

I said, "Al, I have no plans of marrying anyone anytime soon."

Of course, Al's saying it was a Dodger tradition to help out players getting married was pure bullshit. Pedro Guerrero was the next Dodger to get married and he received no Dodger compensation because of it. Al said that was because Pedro had an agent. Well, I had one too, so that argument gets tossed out the window.

Al really disappointed me. I had always liked him a lot. In fairness to Al, however, he was probably just obeying orders from above him in the organization. Ownership put pressure on him to do their dirty work. Walter O'Malley was, without question, engineering Al's plea that I get married. To a girl, of course!

The point I'm trying to make here is that the Dodgers are arguably the sharpest organization in all of sports. They knew I was gay, and were worried about how the average father would feel about taking his son to a baseball game to see some fag shagging fly balls in centerfield. But the fact is, baseball has the same percentage of homosexuals as there is in mainstream society. It's pretty well known in the gay community that within that percentage are two former Most Valuable Players from the seventies. But baseball, perhaps more than any other sport, promotes machismo and virility.

This may come as a shock, but there are more gays in football than any other big-time sport. In the trenches, those guys are like family. They can really get off on the body chemistry. But gay football players, like other gay athletes, fake heterosexuality. They date women, get married. They protect their careers. They protect their ability to be promotable. Someone like tennis legend Martina Navratilova probably lost $10 or $20 million in sponsorships due to her never hiding the fact she is a lesbian. It's just not right.

And I knew all this going in. That's why I tried to live a double life.

When we were on the road, I would wait until my teammates were either in their rooms for the night or out on the town before heading out to gay bars and parties. I would anxiously flag down a taxicab while practically covering my head so no one would notice me. If someone did, I never acknowledged them.

I was even fearful that the cabdrivers would notice I was a ballplayer, so I would always tell them to pull over a block or two from where I was going. No straight dude will ever know how difficult this charade is to play.

One time, back in '77, I was getting into a taxicab and a

teammate did recognize me. He had me dead to rights. He said, "Hey, where are you headed, man? Didn't you say you were staying in tonight?"

I said, "Changed my mind."

He wanted to come along. But I told him he didn't want to go where I was going. I figured it was the safest thing I could possibly respond with. On one hand, I was telling him I didn't want him to join me. But on the other hand, if he was gay too, then he would figure out what I was saying. And that, of course, would have been the best-case scenario. I would have then had someone to share my thoughts with on being a gay baseball player.

Upon arriving a hundred yards or so from my destination, I would turn my head ninety degrees away from traffic. While I was walking briskly to the gay bar or party, the thought would always run through my head if I was going to meet someone I knew there. Or if someone would snap a picture and try to blackmail me. Or if I was recognized as being the Dodgers' top young prospect, should I deny and pretend I was someone else?

Once in the bar, I would keep one eye on the door at all times. Seriously. I hardly drank anyway, so there was never a danger of getting drunk and revealing who I was. But I did have a temper, and often had to restrain myself from getting into fights that would inevitably draw attention to me.

I became extremely paranoid. Even though I was very careful about concealing my homosexuality, there were more than a few occasions I thought someone from the front office had someone spying on me. And there were also times I was convinced everybody was whispering about Glenn Burke, the in-hiding Dodger homosexual.

While in hiding, I told countless lies to teammates on where I was going. "Just going for a walk," I'd often say.

Some nights, I got so depressed about the lies and deception, I would just sit in my room alone and smoke some weed. For a while, that made me feel better. In '78, I started using cocaine recreationally. That was even better.

Pot and coke are the only two drugs I've ever done.

My drug use as a Dodger shouldn't surprise anyone. Drugs were very available to professional ballplayers in the 1970s and 1980s. In fact, drugs are still very available to big leaguers.

The drug dealers would actually come into the locker room to bring you the drugs. They would act like deliverymen. They all had different disguises and gimmicks in getting the drugs to you. The dealers might walk into the locker room and say, "Hey, how are you doing? Here are the cards you wanted printed up."

Drugs were in every locker room in baseball. Even the locker room of the pristine Dodgers. And when I say every locker room in baseball, I don't just mean major-league baseball. It went on, to a lesser degree, in the minor leagues too. Which brings to mind the rather frightening time I was called up from Triple-A Albuquerque to play for the Dodgers. It should have been a joyous moment, but it certainly didn't start out that way.

With a month and a half to go in that season at Albuquerque

in 1976, I was batting over .300 for the fifth straight season and had stolen sixty-three bases. Lopes had messed up his rib cage, so then–Dodger manager Walter Alston said, "Call up Glenn Burke."

I was in my dormitory room at the time. Because I was on the big-league roster, Jeffrey Leonard was my roommate. Leonard, who would get called up to the Dodgers the next season, would go on to have a great career with the Astros and the Giants. So Leonard, future Cy Young Award winner Rick Sutcliffe, future major-league standouts Ivan De Jesus and Ron Washington, and Albuquerque teammates Cleo Smith and Mike Demo were all in my room playing cards and smoking pot. And we were playing for money.

There was a knock on the door. It was one of the coaches. I said, "Oh shit!"

So we cleared the room as quickly as possible, put Visine in our eyes to clear the red out from all the smoke, and started to spray the room to get rid of the odor.

The coach said, "Mr. Sweppy wants to see you in the mess hall, Glenn Burke. Right away!" Sweppy was the head of the minor leagues.

I was pretty scared. I yelled at the players in my room, "You guys come to my room to play cards and smoke dope, and you take the chance of getting me in trouble. You do it thinking I probably won't get in any trouble. I'm the Dodgers' top prospect, right? Well, look what's happening now."

One of them said, "That's right, Glenn. You are the top prospect. Don't worry about it."

But I was still concerned. I remember thinking, "Hey, you never know. Maybe I am in a lot of trouble."

I got on my bike and went over to the mess hall and was hanging my head practically to the ground. I walked into the room, and there were about forty players, team and league officials. I walked up front, where five minor-league directors sat.

I said, "Mr. Sweppy, you wanted to see me?"

Mr. Sweppy responded by saying what every young kid dreams of hearing. "Glenn, we just wanted to call you up here to let you know you're going to the big leagues!"

In front of scouts, managers, and directors, I said, "You're not fucking with me, are you?"

The place roared with laughter and applause.

Sweppy said no, and asked how long it would take me to get dressed. I said ten minutes. After everyone in the room lined up to congratulate me and shake my hand, I went back to my room.

After all the excitement, I felt a little down. A little angry. I told off the guys who were in my room smoking dope and gambling. I said, "Goddamnit, I'm tired of doing this shit with you guys. It's going to get me in trouble someday."

They said, "Glenn, what's the matter?"

I said, "No, no, I don't want to talk to you guys. There's always a chance of getting in trouble doing this shit. You don't care."

One of them responded with "Burke, you're going to the Dodgers!"

Then it really registered. I smiled and said, "Damn, I'm going to the big leagues!"

They jumped all over my head and poured wine and water on me. De Jesus was hugging me and crying. We were all so happy.

I've done my share of drugs. But I gave away more than I've ever done. I was the one that had the money. I would treat friends to the cocaine. They would say, "Thank you, can my friend have some too?"

I would always say, "Sure."

The friend of the friend would always want to become best buddies with you. Best buddies, that is, until the coke was gone. They said they'd call you up to hang out, but they never did. And I never waited for them to call anyway.

My first big-league game was at, of all places, Candlestick Park. My major-league roller coaster and tumultuous relationship with Tommy Lasorda was about to begin.

Just before game time, I was walking down to the dugout with Dodger relief pitcher Mike Marshall. The Candlestick fans started to boo us. I turned to Mike and asked, "What are they booing me for?"

Mike said, "Glenn, they're booing me. They don't even know who you are."

Nobody around the National League liked Mike Marshall. He always stood on that mound looking ever so intimidating with that big mustache and those glaring looks. But he could get them out.

Late in the game, Alston needed someone to pinch-hit. It was the ninth inning, runners on first and second, and two outs. It was my first major-league at bat. I hit a smash up the middle. But short-stop Chris Speier dove and snared the ball in his glove, then flipped it to second to force Rick Auerbach at second to end the game.

But I did good. I got a good piece of that ball. In appreciation, the Dodgers gave me a watch at the end of the game. I was also interviewed on the Dodger postgame show. I thought to myself, "What a great day. And what a class organization the Dodgers are."

My admiration of the Dodgers at that time only mirrored theirs of me.

"Once we get him cooled down a little from wanting to play all the time," said the late Jim Gilliam, one of the Dodger coaches at the time, "frankly, we think he's going to be another Willie Mays."

"Unlimited potential" is how my buddy Lopes described my abilities as I came on the scene.

Even at the infancy of my big-league career, I may have feared success a little bit. I thought to myself, "Hey, I want to hit over .300 and become a star and a hot commodity, but then the secret could be leaked out. That could be a good thing or a bad one. A good thing if I told anyone with a problem dealing with it to go to hell, a bad one if it got me blackballed from the game despite the success. Perhaps being an average ballplayer and hitting .250 or .260 would be better. That way, it would be easier to guard my privacy. There would be less of a chance of anyone ever finding out."

I had many great relationships with the Dodger players and

coaches. Dusty, Davey, Garvey, Sutton, Gilliam. Even Tommy and I were friends at the beginning.

It was Dusty and Davey who really took an instant liking to me. They said I was a breath of fresh air, the life of the team. Those two were like big brothers to me. They always made sure I wasn't lonesome. They were always trying to set me up with dates. They would give me rides home and ask me if I wanted them to hang around for a while. But, for obvious reasons, I didn't want them to meet my roommate at the time.

Dusty is now a great manager with the Giants. He's a great manager because his guidance to his players comes from the heart. That makes an individual awfully hard to beat. Sometimes, I wonder what Dusty would do if he had a player like me on his current Giants team. I don't necessarily mean the gay part of Glenn Burke, but rather the part of me that would blast music in the clubhouse and say things that would keep the team laughing. With baseball being as serious as it is these days, I like to think he would welcome someone like me to keep things loose. Dusty is a wonderful man. When I was first put into the hospital for AIDS-related complications, Dusty called to check on me. It warmed my heart. He's a busy man, with his managing and everything, and I was thrilled to hear from him.

Lopes is a good man too. He's a real leader and is the perfect coach now for the Baltimore Orioles. We used to call him and shortstop Bill Russell "Frick and Frack." They combined to become one of the longest-running double-play combinations in baseball history. And, for you trivia buffs, the two are, along with Garvey and third baseman Ron Cey, a part of a Dodger infield that holds the all-time record for longevity among infields. I liked Russell too. He was a quiet Oklahoma boy. Cey was a great player but was really wrapped up in himself.

On the road that first year, Bill Buckner and I would hang out. He's strange. He had those big heavy eyebrows. He was a great player. I really enjoyed his company a lot. Maybe because I was kind of strange too.

Rick Monday and I never had a chance. We could never see eye to eye because we were always in competition for the centerfield spot. He gave me a lot of grief. But I didn't care, because I was after his ass. He would fuck with me. Try to keep me off balance. But that shit of his didn't really bother me.

Reggie Smith was an asshole too. He treated me the way Monday treated me. Maybe he saw me as a little bit of a threat as well.

As I mentioned earlier, Garvey and Sutton were great to me. Garvey, if I ever had one, was my idol. That was my nickname for him, "Idol." If he ever ran for political office in California, like he would hint at from time to time, he'd have my vote. Despite what the tabloid press has said about him in recent years, he's a nice man. Period. Anyone who says anything different does not know Steve Garvey. They called him "Mr. Clean," and he was.

Garvey did a lot to help me mature. Like Baker and Lopes, he was like an older brother to me, too. He taught me how to tie a tie, he gave me hats and T-shirts, he sat with me on the team plane, and he made me promise to play for him if he ever had a football team. Garvey, with those infamously developed forearms of his, played freshman football at Michigan State. He'd say, "Glenn, you'll be my fullback when I have a team one day." That made me feel good. The Dodgers' nickname for me was "King Kong," because of my six-two, 220-pound build.

As for Sutton, he was just a likable guy to just about everyone. He had a great personality. He liked to clown around a lot. He used to call me "Toby," after the character from *Roots*. I took it the way it was intended, as a joke. Don was the first one to include me. He'd say on the spur of the moment something like "C'mon Toby, we're going out for drinks." He didn't throw me any shit. He's a nice person, and I'm sure his personality had a lot to do with his landing a job as a baseball commentator. That clown also won over three hundred baseball games.

Of all the coaches, Jim Gilliam was the most influential to me. He would talk to me about life and baseball. We referred to Gilliam as "The Devil," because he simply looked like a little devil. Gilliam kept me out of trouble. He would let me know exactly what time it was. He'd say, "Glenn, you come up here from the minors pouting and shit just because you're not starting. You'll get your chance."

Gilliam's cooling me down was crucial to keeping me out of Tommy's doghouse. I really felt I was good enough to start over Monday. How is a player supposed to feel after hitting over

.300 for five straight professional seasons, then coming up to the big leagues and picking splinters out of his ass? But you realize the politics, the money, and the fact they were paying Monday *big* money. So I had to wait my turn. That was the bottom line.

When I did get a chance, in my first full season in '77, I would come through. I'd get two hits one day, two hits the next, then ride the bench for two weeks. It was hard to get into any kind of groove or zone when I played so irregularly. On one hand, playing for a winning organization like the Dodgers was exciting. Great hitting, great pitching, big crowds all the time. But on the other hand, I wanted to start. Fortunately or unfortunately, however, we had the best outfield in baseball and a lineup that featured four guys—Baker, Smith, Garvey, and Cey—who hit at least thirty homeruns in '77.

Taking that last factor a step further, after Baker's thirtieth homerun gave the Dodgers their fourth player to accomplish that feat, I went into the baseball history books by being credited with giving the very first "high five."

We were playing at Dodger Stadium and Dusty was up before I was. It was his last at bat of the regular season. Baker needed to hit a home run to put the Dodgers in the record books. Big James Rodney Richard, who twice in his career had over three hundred strikeouts in a season, was the pitcher for the Astros. J.R. came in with a pitch to Dusty, and he smashed it into the left-field grandstands for a home run. I was up next and the first player to greet him at home plate. I just put my hand high above my head and he slapped it hard in jubilation, as I shouted, "Way to go! Way to go!"

That was a lot of pressure for Dusty, but he came through like he so often did for the Dodgers. While the crowd stood and cheered for Baker, I followed with the first major-league homerun of my career. The Dodger fans were in a wild frenzy. And as I was heading to the dugout, Baker came out to greet me, and we gave each other the second recorded high five in history.

Nobody had ever seen the high five before. It was not an invention of mine or anything. I just put my hand up there. It's like, you usually shake hands, but Baker hitting his thirtieth home run was something special. I just went above, that's all.

As I touched on earlier, Tommy Lasorda and I were pretty good friends at first. He was a great motivator, who did a great job at getting players pumped up before a game. And he did that in a very comical way. He was a comedian. Very funny and delightful when he wanted to be. He often would take players out to dinner and really made them feel good about themselves.

In my first couple of seasons with the Dodgers, I was always playing practical jokes with Lasorda, always fucking with him in a playful way. I was only with the team a few months when I would merrily barge into his office while he was engaged with some of his Hollywood pals before a game and fix myself a sandwich. They'd look at me incredulously and I would shout with a big grin, "Hi, Tommy!" I did that on more than one occasion.

Another thing I did was to create a wedge between Lasorda

and a player who had just hit a home run. For some reason, Lasorda has never found a handshake to be an adequate enough way to greet a guy after he homers. He has to give him a big hug. He practically mauls the guy. Lasorda clearly does it just to get on camera. He's perfect for L.A. in that respect. So after a Dodger hit a home run, I would stand and cheer, then sprint to Lasorda's end of the dugout, box him out à la Charles Barkley, and I would give out the hugs on camera. The players loved it. And, for a while, Tommy found it kind of amusing.

Another thing I did that made the players roar was my imitations and mimicking of Tommy. I would stuff towels underneath my jersey and walk back and forth in the dugout big-bellied and bowlegged. As long as we kept winning, which we did a lot of in '77 when we were trying to dethrone the two-time defending world champion Cincinnati Reds, Lasorda took it in stride.

But when we'd lose a couple of games or if Monday was in a slump, I tended to get a little antsy. I wanted a real opportunity to play, and the Los Angeles fans and media felt the same way. The fans even began riding Monday. Like I said, I'd have a good couple of games and then sit for two weeks. I would get a little pissed at Lasorda for that. I didn't know his angle in doing that. Maybe he wanted the experience to make me tougher or hungrier. Over time, however, the experience just made me angry. And Lasorda treating me like a kid didn't help. Tommy would bark an order and wanted me to jump like some little boy, just happy for the attention.

In the latter part of '77, he blew his top at me. I was playing one of my little jokes on him, and when some of the guys laughed at it, he didn't take it so well.

"Burke!" screamed Lasorda. "If I was your age, I'd take you in the bathroom right now and kick your ass."

I was hurt. I thought he was joking around with me, but he wasn't. He was pretty pissed. For some reason, I think he was trying to break me, get me to explode.

Lasorda was using me more and more as Monday's ninth-inning defensive replacement. Sometimes, it wasn't even the whole ninth inning. He'd put me out there with one or two outs in the ninth. I'd trot in after the game, and the guys would pop out of the dugout to congratulate us after winning. I felt kind of stupid. After all, I had nothing to do with the win.

So one night I was really pissed about my very limited playing time and just glared at Lasorda for a while to try to piss him off. He took me into the locker room from the dugout and, right in front of Gilliam and another coach, Preston Gomez, cussed me out like I've never been cussed at before. He was yelling mother this and mother that. It was very hurtful. I couldn't help but think his malice toward me had gone deeper than my wanting a chance to play or my practical jokes. Maybe it had to do with my getting along with the other players a bit too well. Or maybe he knew about my close relationship with his gay son, Spunky. Or worse, maybe he knew that I was gay, too.

I have bittersweet memories of Spunky. We were great

friends. He had a tremendous sense of humor. He was a transvestite some of the time, but not all of the time. And extremely flamboyant. The Dodgers always had suspicions that there was a sexual relationship between us. I've never responded to that suspicion. That's my business.

Spunky died of AIDS-related complications a couple of years ago. It's somewhat tragic, but Tommy is still in denial about Spunky's sexual orientation and how he died. He tells his friends Spunky died of pneumonia only, not AIDS complications. I feel bad for Tommy that he lost his son. It must be very painful to bury your child. But he should stop being a jerk and accept Spunky for who he really was.

Spunky and I were a lot alike in many ways and very different in others.

We were alike in that we both were disappointments to Tom because of his homophobia and unwillingness to deal with the whole situation. And because we were both victims of Tommy's in that way, Spunky and I had a bond greater than most.

Another similarity we shared was our sense of humor. As a practical joke, Spunky and I were going to go to Tommy's house one night for dinner, à la the Spencer Tracy–Sidney Poitier movie *Guess Who's Coming to Dinner?* We were going to go to his house wearing pigtails with all the female trimmings. I swear, it was all planned out. Tommy first would have shot us both in the head. Then he would have had a heart attack and died. No question about it. So we chickened out at the last minute.

Spunky and I were different in the sense that I was very masculine and he was very feminine. His flamboyancy was probably a reaction to his father.

Another way we differed was in our preference in geographies. I loved the Bay Area and the Castro in San Francisco, the most populated gay area in the world. Spunky preferred Southern California. But that was cool, because when I played in Los Angeles, it was great to have someone like him to talk to and to go barhopping with. To put it in gay terminology, we enjoyed being "teasing sisters."

I loved Spunky. And it completely shocked me when he didn't want to see me anymore. *Couldn't* see me anymore. The Dodgers had paid him to stay away from me. Spunky was a real pussy to end our friendship like that. A pure pussy! That pussy was just like a woman.

As we were wrapping up the National League Western Division title, building up to a season-ending ten-game lead over the second-place Reds, I would venture to guess a good portion of the team knew about my homosexuality. But because I hadn't admitted to it, much less even been questioned about it, the Dodgers didn't feel compelled to react. It helped that I acted like the "King Kong" tag that had been placed on me instead of the prototypical "sissy" label that most straights recognize homosexuals as.

But the telltale signs were beginning to surface. Some players would ask with a grin, "Is Glenn waiting for his 'girlfriend'?" Or "Don't bend over in the shower, here comes Glenn."

Others would wear towels when they walked to and from the shower and the locker room.

As we began to prepare ourselves to play the Philadelphia Phillies in the 1977 National League Championship Series that fall, leading the double life became a little tougher. I wasn't a superstar, of course, but I was suddenly in the limelight because of the team's success. We were on national television every day now, and without sounding too bold, I was a big handsome guy with a good sense of humor. Girls suddenly were coming out of the woodwork to hang out with me. You know, walk them into parties and clubs. They just wanted to be seen with me. If I had been straight, I would've had a field day. Not only would they wait outside the ballpark or at the hotel, they would try to reach you by phone up at your room. It got to the point where I had to tell the receptionist at the front desk to reject all calls to my room. If I needed to talk to anyone, like my family, I would call them.

I never wanted to mislead women into thinking they had a chance with me. That's why I also thought it was kind of selfish of the Dodger management to ask me to find a girl to marry. How cruel would it have been to marry a girl while having no intentions of ever making love to her? It would have been very cruel. So if I did go out occasionally with a woman, it never involved sex.

Dusty once tried to set me up with his cousin. I knew she was a cute girl, but I told Dusty she was too fat and ugly. It may have been a little strong on my part to say those things, but Dusty never introduced me to any more girls after that experience.

Friends like Dusty were just trying to help me. Whenever any of the other players tried to set me up, I'd always say, "Well, I'll meet her." Then I'd leave her after a few moments. Later, the teammate would ask me what happened. I'd say something like "Well, nothing. You wanted me to meet her, right? I met her."

What were the players going to say to me after that? I was 220 pounds. They're not going to say anything to me. Size helped.

Against the Phillies in the play-offs, we played our asses off. We felt it was our time to shine, especially since we had won the division title over the Reds by ten games.

With Steve Carlton going for the Phillies and Tommy John going for us, we figured we were in for a low-scoring game. It wasn't to work out quite that way. With the Phillies ahead with a comfortable 5-to-1 lead in the seventh, thanks in part to Greg Luzinski's two-run homer, Cey belted a grand slam in our half of the inning to tie it up at five apiece. Cey came out for a curtain call flexing his muscles. He looked like a little superman.

Our great comeback was all for nothing, as the Phillies staged a two-run ninth inning. Singles by Bake McBride, Larry Bowa, and Mike Schmidt off of Elias Sosa saw to that.

We were a little stunned, especially since the loss occurred in our home ballpark. But, on the bright side, anytime you can score five runs against "Lefty," you can't feel too badly about that. And we felt pretty confident the rest of the way in the series, because we definitely had the better pitching staff.

In Game 2, for the second straight day, a Dodger hit a grand slam. This time it was Dusty, my man. The game would be ours, as Sutton scattered nine hits over nine innings for a 7-to-1 victory. It was not only nice to win and tie the series up at a game apiece, but it was extra gratifying to have two of my best friends leading the charge.

The third game, in Philly, was the most thrilling of the series. "Happy" Hooton lasted only an inning and two-thirds, but it wasn't his fault. The home plate umpire must have truly been blind that day. He missed at least ten to fifteen strikes for Hooton, and Hooton was anything but happy about it. He was glaring a hole through that umpire and gave him a piece of his mind after Lasorda pulled Happy out of the game.

We were on the verge of losing, as we were down 5–3 in the top of the ninth with two outs. But we staged an astounding comeback. With Gene Garber, the Phils' closer, on the hill, Vic Davalillo got us going with a single. Manny Mota, possibly the greatest pinch-hitter ever, came off the bench and promptly doubled up the gap to put runners in scoring position. Davey then singled them home, and Russell followed with a game-winning single with Lopes in scoring position. We went wild. There were many high fives that afternoon!

The thing that people should realize about the post-season is that it's the play-offs that are actually far more exciting than the World Series. Sure, you bust your tail to win the World Series, but the finality of a best-of-five series, like the play-offs were then, was much more pressure-packed. After all, very few people can name division champion teams. But everyone remembers who played in the World Series. Even the losing teams.

Tommy John was his old self in Game 4, pitching a complete-game five-hitter, and Dusty smacked another homer, and we won the Championship Series, three games to one. We were, naturally, thrilled by winning the pennant. But we were anxiously awaiting the outcome of the American League Championship between the Yankees and the Royals. We didn't care who we played, because we knew we could beat either one of them. But it's important to know your opponent so you can make plans and strategies.

Ironically, I saw some decent playing time in the Phillies series, but I didn't make the most of it. Carlton owned me with that wicked slider of his, and I went hitless in seven trips. But I was happy for Dusty, who picked up MVP honors for his outstanding play in the series. He hit two home runs, drove in eight, and batted .357 against some good Phillies pitching.

As it turned out, of course, we were to play the Yankees in the 1977 World Series. And I was pretty happy about that. New York's more fun than Kansas City in many ways, and I had never been to Yankee Stadium.

The first thing that really stood out in my mind was all the media attention. I mean, there was just too much of it going on. I had never before been approached by more media than I was in that series. It was almost bizarre some of the questions they'd ask.

The commercialism also stunned me. Because I was going to start in Game 1 with lefty Don Gullett pitching for New York, Puma paid me $300 to wear their brand of spikes.

But as far as all the attention being a distraction, it certainly was not. You could always stay away from it all by shagging flies or taking batting practice.

Personally, I had a pretty good World Series debut. I made a great catch in center field and was involved in the series' most pivotal play. We were leading 2-to-1 in the top of the sixth, and I singled to center field. Yankee center fielder Mickey Rivers, who had a weak throwing arm, threw Garvey out at home trying to score from first base. It set off a big argument at home between Garvey and the home plate umpire before Lasorda joined the mix. We ended up losing the game in twelve innings, 4–3. But I was really pleased that I was able to contribute, especially after going hitless in the championship series.

I didn't see a whole lot more playing time the rest of the series but, then, why should I have? I had a good Game 1, after all, and that fit right in with Lasorda's agenda for me.

We pummeled an injured Catfish Hunter the next night behind four home runs and some great pitching by Hooton. But the 6–1 victory wasn't what I remember from that game. It was those terrible Yankee fans. They were clowns that night. They would throw shit at you. Screws, bolts, anything they could find. We were playing the next three games in L.A. and were going to try our damnedest to win the World Series at Dodger Stadium. I mean, they were animals that night. They even fucked with our cars. That's New York, I guess. Anything is possible there.

And to add fuel to the fire, the New York tabloids were calling us crybabies. Well, I'd like to see one of those writers try to do their job while someone's throwing metal objects at them.

As it turned out, we did have to return to New York. We lost a couple of tough ones in Games 3 and 4, then crushed them in Game 5, winning 10–4 on the power of thirteen hits.

It's funny, but none of us thought anything of it when Reggie Jackson hit a solo home run in the top of the eighth to make it a 10–4 game. The Yankees were still down by six runs, and Sutton would end up cruising through the ninth inning for a complete game victory. But Jackson's home run was a prelude of what would occur in Game 6 two nights later.

I invited a couple of my friends, Manny Simmons and Wes Jackson, to join me on the trip to New York so they could see the World Series at Yankee Stadium. The three of us had a lot in common. We were all gay black men who loved sports and really worked hard at staying in shape together.

Manny was a tremendous athlete. He was an All Southeast Asia track star while in the service and played football at Azusa Pacific. Azusa is now famous for having Christian Okoye, the great football player, as one of its alumni.

Wes played baseball and football at Cal State Hayward, which is across the San Francisco Bay.

I knew them both from the YMCA and, of course, the Castro. We were all just buddies. I took them down to the field and through the locker room. Everyone on the team went out of their way to make them feel comfortable. Everyone, except Reggie Smith. Reggie, despite hitting three home runs for us in the World Series, was still an asshole.

We took a 2–0 lead in the first off Mike Torrez, but after Chris Chambliss tied it with a home run in the Yankee second, Mr. October took over. Jackson hit the next three successive pitches to him out of the park to seal the game and the series for the Yankees.

As Jackson circled the bases after hitting his third home run of the game, a tremendous shot into the center-field bleachers, I had tears in my eyes. Not because we were going to lose the World Series. I cried because I was happy for him. Reggie was an all right guy and that was a tremendous individual feat. Growing up in Oakland, I got to see him play a lot. Reggie was a great power hitter.

Garvey was happy for him too. He said later he was clapping his right hand in his glove for Reggie. You just couldn't help but be in awe of Jackson's achievement.

The day after the World Series, I bought two things to remember my series appearance with. The first was a great idea, a new Volkswagen. Drove it right out of the showroom window. The second wasn't the best of all ideas. I got a tattoo of a scorpion, my sign. I went down to this place called Bob Smith's on Hollywood Boulevard. Getting that tattoo hurt like the motherfucker. I promised myself I would never do that again. I went in Bob Smith's and said, "Give me a little tatoo." That bitch started drilling in my arm, and I said, "Wait a minute. How long is this going to take? Maybe I'll change my mind!" But there was no turning back. And I'm glad I did it. You can never get rid of a tattoo, and I've always had that scorpion to remind me of being in the World Series.

Getting traded to the A's should have been a great chance for me to shine. And it sure started out that way, as I got three hits in my American League debut. But, with the exception of Mitchell Page and a couple other players, that team had no spirit. Just as good baseball breeds good baseball, the same can be said for bad baseball. The A's owner, Charlie Finley, had seen to that. They didn't have a single guy left from their glory days, which were from only two or three years before. I ended up hitting a disappointing .235, as the team lost 93 games.

The following year was even worse, as the A's went on to lose 108 games. A pinched nerve, depression over the lack of spirit on that team, and the strain of living my double life led me to voluntarily retire well before the season was over. I needed a break from it all.

Enter Billy Martin in 1980. I knew things would change in Oakland for the better with Billy at the helm. He had won two pennants with the Yankees and seemingly got the most out of his players. I was excited to see the A's finally doing something to try and improve themselves. I decided to come out of retirement. I felt I was still young and had a lot of years left to play ball. And, most importantly, my mind was finally back together from that fiasco with the Dodgers. The decision to play for Billy, however, turned out to be a bad one. The day I arrived for Spring Training, Martin started telling people behind my back that "no faggot" was going to play on one of his teams.

I was crushed and decided to leave the A's permanently. I was leaving the A's because of Billy Martin. I wasn't going to go through that homophobic shit with another manager. I didn't need that over my head again. What would have made it even worse was the fact Martin went to the same high school I did. He potentially could have really tried to ruin me.

Martin never called me a faggot to my face. He may have known I would've kicked that ass.

It was all caving in on me. The Dodgers knew my secret. Now the A's.

I waited two years for a call from a team. Only one team, the Pirates, inquired about my availability. And the Pittsburgh scout asked my pal, Mitchell Page, if I was bisexual.

My life as a baseball player was over. Because I was a homosexual, no team was ever going to give me a real chance to play the game I loved. And baseball had stripped me of my inner thoughts. I would now begin the second phase of my life, a single life, as a gay man.

2

THE MINOR LEAGUES

knew I was different. I wasn't dating either men or women. Sex just wasn't a part of my life. Period. It just wasn't important to me. I didn't want to have sex with anyone.

So I used all of my energy and aggression toward playing baseball. And as long as I hit .300, as I did five straight seasons in the minors, nobody could say shit to me. By devoting all of my energies and drive toward the game—I'm convinced it made me a better player. So I'm awfully glad I didn't have any interference.

I would still go out and party with teammates. But I was bigger than everybody. So no one ever pushed me into anything I didn't want to do. My size helped. I was around 220 pounds then. They called me King Kong. I was built like a tank.

In addition, I kept moving up through the ranks, so the vast majority of the players and management never really got to know me that well. They never questioned why I didn't have the outwardly sexual drive of the average ballplayer.

My professional baseball career began in Ogden, Utah. To say the least, Ogden never was and never will be a hotbed for young gay blacks. Although, at the time, I still didn't realize I was gay. Ogden's a beautiful area of the country, but there was quite a bit of racism at that time. Two incidences stick out.

When I first went to Ogden, I went to a local restaurant to have something to eat. It wasn't very crowded, but the waitress kept me waiting for half an hour, and that bothered me. I said to the waitress, who was named Carolyn, that I deserved the same service as anybody else. After all, it was 1972, not 1952.

Carolyn said, "Oh, I'm sorry. I didn't know you were one of the ballplayers. My apologies. I was really busy."

Carolyn served me immediately. After I left, she came by my table to pick up my plate to find I had left her a thirteen-cent tip.

A few days later I went back to the restaurant to have some lunch, and again Carolyn was my waitress. I said, "How are you doing today, ma'am?"

All she could say was "I apologize again about not serving you the other day."

I knew she was full of shit. So I ran her. I must have called for her assistance four or five times, asking for ketchups, mustards, water, you name it. If there was anything in that kitchen, I sent her for it. To punctuate how I felt, I again left her a thirteen-cent tip. But that was it. I had made my feelings known and it was over.

....

Another time, I was walking down an Ogden street with Cleo Smith and Marvin Webb, two teammates of mine who ironically were both from the Bay Area. Cleo went to Kennedy High in the Oakland area, Marvin was from Richmond, and I attended Berkeley High. We had met playing high school ball against one another. Well, on this particular day, the Mormons were on the street preaching the gospel according to them. It was kind of like today when a Muslim walks up to you and says, "Have you got the latest, brother?"

The Mormons were saying, "Why don't you buy one of these *Mormon Speaks?*"

When we very nicely said, "Thanks, but no thanks," this one Morman erupted.

The Morman said, "Well, you blacks are the cause of all the problems in the world."

Marvin said, "Man, you better get away from me."

As the incident began to be perpetuated, I could feel the steam rising to my head. I started toward the clown, who was only about twenty years old, about my age at the time. Thank God Cleo and Marvin stopped me, or I would've kicked that boy's ass all over the street.

Needless to say, I didn't buy one of his *Morman Speaks.*

Marvin and Cleo became lifelong friends of mine. Marvin and I would end up playing four years of minor-league ball together. When I first went to Ogden, Marvin, Cleo, and I stayed in a hotel called the Ben Loman. I could never understand why Marvin never made the big leagues. I'm sure there was some racism involved in keeping Marvin down. We often battled for the highest averages on our way up the minor-league ladder, and he always performed well in Spring Training games against major-league pitchers. Marvin consistently had between thirty and forty doubles a year in the minors. Once, while playing in A ball, in the Carolina League in 1974, Marvin got three hits in that league's all-star game. So how did his team reward him for excelling in the spotlight? They started a white player hitting .232 ahead of him. Marvin would go as high as Triple A with Albuquerque, playing with such future stars as Pete Guerrero, Rick Sutcliffe, Dave Stewart, and Rudy Law, but he was unmercifully sent to the Mexican League. After participating in the Inter-America League, which included such sites as Panama and Santo Domingo, for a team managed by Davey Johnson called the Miami Amigos, he was finished in baseball. The Inter-America League folded after just two months.

"Marvelous" Marvin was robbed.

Nicknames were as popular in the minors as the two-and-oh fastball. I was primarily just called King Kong, but some guys like Marvin had more than one. Besides Marvelous, which the kids practically demanded he use when signing a baseball, he was also referred to by the fans and media alike as "The Marvelous Doctor M," "Short Dog," or "The Hammer." The nicknames basically summed up Marvin as a toy cannon-like hot dog. But unlike so many others, Marvin could back up his showboating with a ton of talent on the diamond.

In Pittsfield, where we both would play later on in our minor-league careers, they had an all-team for seemingly anything. They had an All Hot Dog Team, an All Pretty Boy Team, and an All Munchkin Team to name a few. Of those very honorable Double-A all-teams, I qualified for the Hot Dog Team. Marvin qualified for all three!

Other than the all-team boards, there wasn't a whole lot more entertaining in Pittsfield for us. The big thing for us was to just get to the ballpark and play ball. We only had to play against Pittsfield for about a year anyway.

Of all the cities I played minor-league ball in, Spokane was probably the most beautiful. Being from Berkeley, I like that atmosphere with shady trees and big houses. It was a low-key place, with many outdoor activities. I actually learned how to water-ski there. It took me four hours to learn, and at first it scared me half to death, but eventually I got the hang of it. The people were also some of the friendliest I've ever met.

The environment must have also helped my ball playing. After playing part of the summer of '72 in Ogden and hitting only .200, I flourished in Spokane, with a .340 batting average in over 140 at bats. Spokane was a nice, all-around experience for me.

Looking back on all my friends, it's truly amazing how Marvin paralleled my athletic life. Not only did we play baseball and basketball against each other in high school, but our mothers had been close friends for years. We were both drafted out of school to play professional baseball, Marvin with the San Diego Padres, me with Los Angeles; Marv held out for a higher signing bonus to play in the Dodger organization. Then, along with Cleo, we went on to become teammates for several years in the minors.

Marvin was quite a lady's man. He used to bring me women when we both played for Daytona Beach in 1973. He would try so hard to get me laid. One time, he was in bed with two women and he shouted for me to come into the bedroom to join in the activities. I said to Marv, "Are you through yet?"

Marv said, "Come on in here, because I'm not through yet! Do you want some or what?"

"Nah, nah, nah, nah" was all I could say.

Another time he brought up a couple more girls from West Palm Beach for us. But this time I made sure I wasn't around when they arrived at our apartment. So, again, Marvin had to be with both of them. He couldn't have been too pissed off at me.

Marvin was relentless. He just thought I was picky as far as women went. After that '73 season, we went to play ball in Arizona. This time, Marv had truly outdone himself. He brought around these two gorgeous girls. And the one Marv introduced to me as my "date" really took a liking to me. She was damned near what any red-blooded straight male would look for in a woman. We were all sitting at the table talking when I just got up and said I had to leave.

Marvin couldn't believe I was leaving and said forcefully, "Oh man! Don't leave!"

I just excused myself from them and left.

Marvin told the girls, "Well, he's a funny kind of guy. Just a funny kind of guy."

I think Marvin and I were discovering at about the same time that there was just no hope for me with women. Perhaps he knew I was gay before I realized it.

Marvin and I enjoyed instant success in Daytona Beach. Through the month of June, three months into the season, we were both hitting over .400. Our names would flip-flop for most of the season as the number 1 and 2 leading hitters in the Florida State League. That damned Florida heat slowed us down a little toward the end of the season, but I ended up hitting .309, and averaged a home run every eleven at bats. I was a power-hitter with speed.

It was also a tumultuous year in some respects. I was fighting battles with team management as well as on the ball field. Our general manager at Daytona Beach, a guy we only really knew as "Sanchez," was withholding our checks on several occasions. So I figured I'd be the team's representative and put a stop to it once and for all. I went to the office building Sanchez worked out of and began yelling for him from the first-floor lobby. Sanchez worked on the second floor. We were paid so little money in those days, barely enough to eat, and I was pissed at how petty ownership was being. So I just kept shouting, "Sanchez! Sanchez! Sanchez! Bring me my motherfucking check!"

It caused quite a commotion, but I got my check almost instantly. I think the other players received theirs soon after as well. As a twenty-year-old kid, I think I earned everyone's respect.

I also used intimidation with the coaches. One time I stole third base with two outs and the Daytona coach, Bart Shirley, told me if I ever did that again, he'd take me out of the game. I turned to him and said, "Yeah, and if you do, I'm going to kick your ass!"

Shirley just turned away and said, "Oh."

I really wasn't trying to show Shirley up, I was just aggressive. I loved playing hard. I was just a bull with a mind of my own.

Larry Parish would go on to become an all-star third baseman with the Montreal Expos. But as a minor leaguer, he'll always remember the name Glenn Burke.

One night in Daytona Beach, I hit one up the gap in left center field and was chugging for third. As I slid into third safely with a triple, Larry thought I'd spit on him. I hadn't, but he started talking shit. The dugouts clear out and both teams were kind of in a circle around Larry and me, ready to brawl. I just ripped off my shirt, buttons flying everywhere.

I yelled at Parish, "See, I'm a big man too!"

Then another future major-league all-star, Parish's teammate Ellis Valentine, starts walking toward me. I looked him square in the eye and said, "What are you going to do, nigger?!"

The comment was intended to embarrass Valentine, but it became somewhat comical when a couple of white guys on the other team remarked, "At least Burke's not talking to us."

Everybody left the scene of the crime after that. Most brawls, especially in baseball, are pretty stupid.

The next season, on a similar play at third, Parish and I got into it again. This time, however, it got ugly. It became a full-fledged brawl between our two teams. I was now with Waterbury, and we were playing the Expos' Double-A team in Quebec. The Expos blamed me, but someone else on our team must have landed a solid punch on Parish. The blow broke his jaw, and Parish had to have it wired up for three to four months.

The guys that knew and played with me knew I wasn't really a violent person. I would only fight if provoked or if someone else needed defending. I was kind of like "The Enforcer" that way.

When I was twenty or twenty-one, I was a very fun-loving sort. My friends nicknamed me "Eddie MacElroy." Back in the early seventies, comedians like Rudy Ray Moore and Richard Pryor would record records that would always include fictional characters in their routines. So my friends and I would listen to and memorize the funny stories Moore would tell about Eddie MacElroy. I did the best impersonations of Moore telling his jokes, so people started calling me "Eddie."

It became a good cover for me in the years to come, as "Eddie" was known as a lady's man.

"Eddie MacElroy," went a line, "brings the women joy!"

So between Eddie and my physique, no one really questioned my manhood.

Overall, that first year in Waterbury was very challenging on the field. Their was a big difference between the rookie leagues and Double-A. I struggled a bit at first in Waterbury, hitting only .248 in a third of a season, but really picked things up when I was moved to the Dodgers' Bakersfield farm team for the rest of the season. Maybe it was the change in climate, but I found my power stroke and batted .338 in the final four months of that 1974 summer. And I'm not just joking about that change in climate. In Waterbury, everything's wet. It's like a moist wet. The ball hardly ever travels. One of the few things I liked about the Waterbury area was the castles. They have some beautiful castles in that area of New England.

Things were looking bright as I looked forward to the off-season. I had just finished a third season of hitting over .300 and had earned a big-league contract. I had been playing under a minor-league contract before '74. The money was significantly better now, but that was just a part of the package. I was given my big-league jersey, which was made of light fabric. While playing under a minor-league contract, I sweated my balls off wearing heavy cottons. My shit didn't stink anymore now! I was in!

Perhaps it was my security as a professional ballplayer that pushed me into looking at the rest of my life. My personal life.

That next season in Waterbury, 1975, I realized my homosexuality. I was twenty-three at the time and wanted to begin my life as a gay man, albeit a closeted one. I wanted to find a junior high school teacher friend of mine that I thought I might have had a crush on as a fourteen-year-old. The teacher's name was Mr. Mendler, and he taught glee club, drama, and work studies. I could never get him out of my mind. I guess I had a crush on him all those years, but never acted upon it. We were just really good friends in junior high, and I liked walking his dog and having long conversations with him. So I called one of my sisters back in Oakland and asked if Mr. Mendler was still teaching at the junior high school. When she confirmed that he was teaching her English class, I zoomed out to Oakland the first opportunity I had.

I had my first sexual experience with Mr. Mendler almost immediately after seeing him again. After the experience, I cried for four hours. I was practically hyperventilating. The tears weren't from guilt, they were from relief. I was relieved because for the first time I was sure of who I was. I had never been able to understand why the other guys at school got so strange when they'd fall in love with some girl from school. I would think to myself, "I'm missing that feeling."

So when I found that "loving" feeling, it was very emotional. I wasn't a hound. I was very sensitive back then. And the fact that Mr. Mendler was older helped me out a lot too. I've always liked older people. I've hung with older people all of my life.

Mr. Mendler and I didn't become steady partners or anything like that. I would go and see him every now and then. I just wasn't that sexually oriented at the time.

I knew I was going to have to make changes in my life to continue my homosexual lifestyle while staying in the closet. I knew even then that "coming out" would be baseball suicide. One of the things I had to do was get my own place. At the time, I was living in a house with Jeff Leonard, Cleo, Marvin, and Eddie Carroll, who was a white pitcher from Orange

County. They all really liked me and wanted me to live with them. I liked them too, but I kept saying to myself, "I'm not going to be around here. I'm going to stay at the YMCA."

I stayed at the YMCA for a month and a half, until the guys all had places of their own. Then I left the YMCA for my own place. The YMCA was a nasty place to live. It was just filthy. There was dirt and blood all over the halls. But it was a perfect cover for me because they had hoops there and everyone knew how much I loved basketball. So they all bought my reasoning. Except maybe Marvin.

Marvin had come to visit me at the Y when Mr. Mendler was there to visit with me for a weekend. After I introduced them to one another, Marv noticed the little cot and gave me kind of a confused look like, "Where's Mr. Mendler going to sleep?"

But to Marvin, or a few other friends who may have figured me out, my homosexuality didn't affect the friendship. Marvin said to me not long after the incident, "I don't care what you are or what you did with Mr. Mendler, you're still my friend."

Saying things like that is one thing, but following through with what you say is another. Marvin was true to his word. He still drove me to and from the games in his new car. And we still went out to clubs together, played basketball at the Y, and he still offered to have me live with him at his split-level apartment. He was intelligent enough to know I wasn't going to make a move on him.

Letting Marvin, a heterosexual, become privy to my new

life was of tremendous comfort to me. He was never judgmental, although I knew some things made him feel very awkward.

One night after a game, Marvin wanted to hang out with me and one of my new friends. We were going to a gay club, so I thought as quickly as I could for an excuse I could give to Marvin to discourage his joining us.

"We're just going shopping," I said.

"Shopping?!" Marvin asked. "At eleven thirty at night!"

"Yeah."

"Well, why don't you bring me back something, because, man, whatever you're going to get must be good!"

A couple of nights later, Marvin was not to be denied. He said, "Glenn, I don't care where we go. I'm coming out with you."

I took Marvin and this guy from Chico, Nick Bobbinger, to a place in downtown Waterbury. The club was dark and had a kind of sweet smell to it. Marvin was pumped at first, thinking it must have been one of those hard rock, Jimi Hendrix–type joints. But then, suddenly, it dawned on Marv that there was something very different about this club from those he had ever frequented before.

To our right were two men checking us all out. To the left were a couple of women kissing in the corner. The girls actually shocked Marvin.

"Glenn! Glenn! Look at those girls!"

I was like, "Uh-huh."

"Glenn, I can't talk to these women. I'm taking off."

So Marvin and Nick left without any hard feelings. My homosexuality was now truly confirmed for Marvin, the first of my friends to know that side of me. But it was no detriment to our relationship.

Nothing should ever come between true friendship and nothing ever did with my friends.

I knew my secret was safe with Marvin. Even still, leading a double life was a challenge right from the beginning for me.

I used to go to this bar in Waterbury called the Road House Cafe. As I was leaving there one night, someone in management for the Waterbury Dodgers saw me coming out. We didn't exchange words, but I gave him one of those looks that said, "Well, I know you're going to tell."

But he never said a word to anyone. Turns out he was just as "guilty" as I was. He would've gone into the Road House Cafe if I wasn't there. It was obvious to me that guy was a closet homosexual himself. And if he ever said anything to anybody, I'd be right back in his face, saying, "Hey, you were there too. Yeah, kissing some man."

So, I figured I was pretty safe.

However, I also remember thinking that in the event that I was wrong about him, that he was following me or something, the confrontation should ignite me to play better. I said to myself, "I'm just going to have to hit .300 and lead the league in steals. Then nobody can say shit to me."

The experience actually made me a better ballplayer.

Waterbury was a trip. It was actually a pretty good place to be homosexual. During that summer of 1975, I fell in love. I must have had a thing for intelligence because, again, this lover's profession was that of teacher. Actually, Alan was a professor at Yale. I used to catch a bus every day to New Haven to be with him. I'd meet him almost always at the Green over by Yale University. We would go to the park, eat and talk. Just like a normal couple. It was excellent! I loved that man so much. He would be my partner for my remaining days in Waterbury, until I was called up to Triple-A Albuquerque the following year. We cried like two little kids the day I left Waterbury.

He said, "I know you're not coming back."

All I could tell him was "I can only go where my baseball sends me."

We kept in touch, and after my playing days with the Dodgers, he came to visit me one time. He teaches nutrition now.

I had begun to form a profile of the type of man that I liked to be partners with. The man was older than me, usually by at least ten years. In addition, he was intelligent and very mature. I never liked playing games like "high wire" in my relationships. I always figured, "Who needs the aggravation?"

I started to really come into my own on the ball field in that '75 season. I think my having a steady, everyday companion contributed to that success. I had resolved many issues within myself.

I led the league in stolen bases and hit twelve home runs as the lead-off hitter. And half of those home runs started off a game. That was the best feeling in the world. It would be like, "Here's the first pitch of the game, and BOOM, we're ahead!"

My style of play then was very similar to that of Rickey Henderson, who now plays for the Oakland A's. Henderson holds the all-time major-league record for home runs to start a game *and* the record for most stolen bases in a career.

Like Rickey, my flashy style of play brought me a degree of contempt from the opposition.

David Clyde was once a number one draft choice of the Texas Rangers before they brought him up to the big leagues in 1973. Highly touted as a minor leaguer, he never achieved the success that Texas had hoped he would on the major-league level, and he ended up at Triple-A Pittsfield in 1975. Needless to say, he was pretty pissed at how his rising star had fallen. And one night in Pittsfield, I didn't help his cause when I slammed doubles in my first two plate appearances against him. The third time up, the inevitable happened. Clyde fired a fastball right at my hip. He threw from the left hand side, so I had little chance of getting out of the way. The ball hit me square on the side, and I dropped in what "appeared" to be total agony. In a way I was lucky he didn't hit me in the groin, because I never wore a cup. Cups always would give me a rash. I was just always careful to keep my glove in front of the "jewelry box."

So after being hit, I fell to the ground and dropped the bat like I was in total agony. The trainer came out to me with "freeze" and had me walk a couple of steps. So I started walking and then fell to the ground again. The crowd, in unison, made this long "Ahhhhh" sound. But I was faking the whole injury.

I had fooled everybody. The trainer gave me another spray. Our coach in the dugout was around asking, "Who can we put in, who can we put in for Burke?"

Besides my ultimate goal of deceiving Pittsfield into thinking I was badly injured, I was fucking with our coach too. He was a chump, and it was fun to watch him panic a little bit over my injury.

I told the coach and trainer that I was all right and wanted to stay in the game as I hobbled over to first base.

To everyone's amazement, on the very first pitch, I took off and stole second base. I stole that base so easily. Pittsfield was so decoyed by my "performance" that I was brushing shit off my uniform before the ball finally arrived at second base. It was my revenge for Clyde throwing at me like he did. And it was the best revenge I knew of. I mean, I could have sat there on the ground after being hit, fighting and cussing at him. But what would that have really accomplished?

There was no reason to hit me just because I got a couple of doubles. What if I had struck out four times? Then I'd have had to make that long walk back to the dugout with fans shouting stuff about my mother and throwing shit. I mean, those fans on the road can be sons of bitches. And your home fans can be tough on you as well if you don't hit. But you've got to blank that shit from your mind. You have to stay within yourself and know how to handle the abuse.

The next pitch, I stole third in a cloud of dust. I just looked over at Clyde as I dusted myself off, with a stare that said, "If you say anything, I'll steal home too, spikes high!"

That was the way I played. I always tried to turn the negative stuff into something positive. But if I hadn't gained revenge like I did immediately after he hit me with the pitch, I would've thought about it too much and it would've burned inside of me. So stealing second and third right away made the pain of that "purpose pitch" go away.

My approach on the ball field that season earned me a promotion to Triple-A Albuquerque in 1976. And I made the most of it. I used my power and speed to its fullest potential and drove in fifty-three runs from the leadoff spot, while stealing sixty-three bases with six weeks still remaining in the season. But I gladly sacrificed those final six weeks to play for the Dodgers in "The Show."

Marvin stayed behind in Waterbury, as did my professor friend, Alan. They were two of the most important people in my life. But while I would think about them often, my career was taking off. And that, obviously, was my objective.

I was reunited with Cleo at Albuquerque, which was great. I was always fortunate to have played with either Cleo or Marvin for most of my way through the minor-league ranks.

We had one helluva team, with Leonard, Sutcliffe, De

Jesus, and others. The Dodgers had, and still have, the finest farm system on the planet. They've always pumped out one Rookie of the Year after another, going all the way back to the forties and fifties.

And now, after my fifth straight season of hitting .300 or better in the Dodger organization, I would get my chance to be a Rookie of the Year.

3

EARLY RETIREMENT

The names rang out like a roll call at Cooperstown. Reggie. Vida. Catfish. Rollie. Campy. Rudi. In a span of five years, from 1971 through 1975, the Oakland A's won their Western Division every season. And in three of those years, from '72 through '74, they won the World Series. Combine that with the great success of the Oakland Raiders and the Bay Area was truly the Home of Champions during that period.

With the depth of talent the A's had during those years, anybody would have figured them to easily stay competitive for years to come. But by 1977, just two years removed from their glory days, the A's were a last-place team. And when the A's dealt Billy North to the Dodgers for me the following season, all twenty-five roster players from their 1975 Western Division–winning team were gone!

So when I was traded from the defending National League champion Dodgers to an A's team that was raped of all their talent by free agency and a cheap owner named Charlie Finley, my feelings were pretty mixed up. On one hand, I looked at it as a break. No longer would I have to worry about playing time. Shit, with the Dodgers, I was always looking over my shoulder because I was afraid Tommy was going to take me out. I didn't have to think about kissing anybody's ass anymore. And the A's didn't know I was gay, so I would get a fresh start in that department. Plus, I was going home.

On the other hand, I was pissed. I liked playing for a winner. And Dodger Stadium and the fans were beautiful. The A's, however, had a very universal stadium with hardly any fans left. And who could blame the fans that didn't come anymore? People think right away about Andy Messersmith and Dave McNally as being the first to reap the rewards of free agency. Well, you could also make that same statement about the core of the entire Oakland A's ball club, as well. Bert Campaneris went to Texas. Sal Bando to Milwaukee. Reggie Jackson to Baltimore (then to the Yankees for really big bucks). Joe Rudi to California. Catfish Hunter to the Yankees. Vida Blue to San Francisco. And Rollie Fingers to San Diego. Charlie Finley, with his pettiness, had single-handedly fucked an entire generation of Oakland fans.

Don't get me wrong: players can be greedy too. Today, if a player hits .265, he feels like he deserves a million bucks a year.

That's insane. But those motherfuckers won three straight World Series, and Finley wouldn't give them raises! That man just sold out.

The Dodgers just never gave me a chance. They blackballed me, and that fact still bothers me to this day. Little did they know who else was gay in the baseball world. And it wasn't even like I was some flaming homosexual. You would never know by my demeanor that I could be gay. I never threw my orientation in anyone's face. It was nobody's business. I guess Tommy just couldn't stand me being friendly with his son Spunky. Nor could he stand the fact that, at a young age, I could bust my other teammates into laughter partially at Tommy's expense. It was all in fun, but he took it as some fucking power play. But I'm not bitter. Bitterness doesn't solve shit. I remember thinking that the Dodgers didn't give me a chance to be the next Willie Mays. But maybe the A's would.

It was kind of ironic, but the day I was to make my A's debut, I learned that my center-field nemesis with the Dodgers, Rick Monday, was going to be on the bench indefinitely because of a pulled thigh muscle. But I didn't let that bother me. It was something I couldn't control, so I focused instead on the game at hand against the Chicago White Sox at the Oakland Coliseum.

We were actually in first place at the time, but the Oakland fans were probably still pissed at Finley. Only 5,515 fans showed up on a beautiful May evening in the Bay Area. Wilbur

Wood, the legendary knuckleballer, was pitching for the White Sox.

Despite losing the game, I had made my presence felt. I went 3-for-5 in my debut in probably my only good memory as an Oakland A's player. I was pumped because I was out to show the Dodgers they had made a mistake in trading me.

In my first at bat that night, I lashed a double to the left-field corner, setting up Mitchell Page's run-scoring infield hit. I also had a couple of singles. But I also took part in a bizarre at bat that ended the game. We were down 5–2 with Jim Willoughby in to relieve Wood and one out in the ninth. There were two runners on, and I represented the tying run at the plate. I had gone 3-for-4 against Wood and was sorry to see him leave, but I was pumped at the prospect of hitting in such a key spot. I hit a grounder to third, which third baseman Eric Soderholm threw to second baseman Jorge Orta for the first out, but our Steve Staggs crashed into Orta to prevent a throw to first. Second-base umpire Jim McKean called me out at first, enforcing a new rule practically eliminating the take-out slide. McKean claimed Staggs had "grabbed" Orta, which he hadn't, but there wasn't much any of us could do about it.

We made a lot of mental and physical mistakes in that loss, and I thought to myself, "How in the world is this team in first place? A lot of these guys don't have their heads in the game." The first-place standing wouldn't last for very much longer.

Team spirit is so vital in the big leagues. You begin in mid-

February for Spring Training and play thirty-something games. Then you play 162 regular season games, going from city to city every five days or so. If you make the play-offs and World Series, it's another three weeks before the season finally wraps itself up at the end of October. That team spirit has got to start from the top of the organization. Despite my problems with the Dodgers, that team had a great attitude toward winning. Bobby Winkles and Charlie Finley would never be confused with Tom Lasorda and Walter O'Malley. The A's clearly had no spirit at all. Only Mitchell Page showed the desire I had been used to seeing with the Dodgers. And his numbers followed through with that desire, as he led the team in batting, home runs, and RBIs.

As a result of the poor attitude, Winkles was fired and replaced by Jack McKeon. The move didn't help, as we finished the season with ninety-three losses. Depressed by the whole situation, I hit only .235. I made the mistake of being brought down by the rest of the players. I guess if winning's contagious, so is losing.

No one realized it at the time, but as Oakland A's players, we were in the presence of greatness. Our batboy was later to be known as MC Hammer, one of the today's most recognized rap stars. I think he refers to himself now as just plain old "Hammer." He was such a skinny little kid, with a really low, confident voice. He told me he got his nickname from Hank Aaron because they looked so much alike. That boy was a breath of fresh air in that clubhouse. He was a good kid and I'm happy about all the success he has today. And I'm also impressed with how he's always thanking the Lord for blessing him with all he's accomplished. He apparently never lost his humility.

For as bad as things were for the A's in 1978, it would turn out to be a picnic compared to the 1979 season. I wasn't around for the completion of that nightmare, but the team would end up losing 108 games. Jim Marshall, my third A's manager in less than a year, would be out of a job when the season ended.

Charlie Finley had embarrassed baseball before, but he had truly outdone himself in dismantling any talent we had left. Anyone who played well would either be traded or benched until they attained free-agent status. We had very few hitters of major-league ability and not many capable fielders, either. Our young pitchers were the only bright spot, but we figured they'd be gone soon too if Charlie could swing a two-for-one deal for them.

The fact was, we were losing for winning. And it was clearly going to remain that way until Charlie sold the team. We'd finish the season with a .239 team batting average, with four of our starters hitting .233 or less. In the field, we committed the second most errors in all of baseball, with only the Atlanta Braves finishing with more. The writers began referring to us as "baseball's boat people"!

Personally, I had a horrible year almost from the beginning. I suffered a severe pinched nerve in my neck but was forced to play anyway. Charlie would say to me, "Son, if you get a cortisone shot, you'll be feeling much better."

Charlie liked to call his ballplayers "son." At least it wasn't "boy"! I didn't get the cortisone shot because I felt my body was trying to tell me something with all the pain. My body was saying, "Give me a rest. Give me some time to heal naturally."

Charlie, however, didn't want any part of what my body was telling me. He had me benched the following two weeks.

You know, I still feel that way about shots and pills. Once you get started with those things you start becoming dependent on them.

Benching me was Finley just being Finley. He would run a young player into the ground if he could, even if that meant risking permanent damage. But when it got to the point when my batting average had slipped down to .213 by May, I ended up benching myself. It was a hard thing to do because I was very competitive back then. But I certainly wasn't helping the team by playing hurt to the extent that I was.

Even though Finley was looking to cash out and sell the club, he still loved the power aspects about his position. He would actually play manager all the time, calling down to the dugout with lineup changes on a regular basis. It drove our managers crazy.

My secret appeared to be pretty safe up in Oakland, four hundred miles removed from my troubles in Los Angeles. Although, in certain situations in other cities, I was beginning to have my doubts. There was a time in Chicago's Comiskey Park, in a game against the White Sox, when a fan yelled out to me in the outfield and called me a faggot. Maybe the fan called all the opposing center fielders faggots, but I was so paranoid then about my double life, I really wasn't sure what to think.

Then there was the article written by a columnist in the *San Francisco Chronicle* saying there was rumored to be a local professional baseball player who could be found on Castro Street, the gay section of the city.

It was all beginning to cave in on me.

Besides the anxiety of keeping my double life a secret, I was becoming increasingly depressed over the situation with the hapless A's and my injury. I also felt that I was depriving myself of my true homosexual life by living a double one. I felt it would be a matter of time before someone on the A's found out about my homosexuality and I'd be in the same boat as before. So later that month, I voluntarily retired from baseball. I was tired of all the bullshit.

My friends, who probably didn't fully understand what I was going through, were shocked. They never got down on me about it, but they were so surprised that my promising career was over. They just didn't see it coming because I had never quit anything in my entire life. After all, I still hadn't reached my potential as a hitter, although I had shown my abilities in the field and on the base paths.

The time off to think and to heal my injury put me in a renewed state of mind when it was Spring Training time in 1980. I wanted to play ball again. I was healthy and felt the time out of the spotlight helped conceal my double life. And I felt I had something to prove in regards to my professional goal of becoming a major-league all-star.

Incredibly, it seemed like the A's were actually making moves to improve themselves. And it started at the top. Billy Martin, who was fired from the Yankees in the off-season for punching out some marshmallow salesman, was now the skipper. Apparently, the Yankee owner, George Steinbrenner, was willing to pay something like half of Billy's salary even though he'd be managing in Oakland. It made sense to me, because Charlie would never have shelled out the bucks himself for someone of Billy's talent. I was pumped about having Martin as a manager because I knew that he wouldn't put up with the bullshit we had the last couple of seasons. Billy had one of the best winning percentages in baseball history as a manager and had won division championships in Minnesota, Detroit, and New York. He was a fighter, going all the way back to his days when he went to Berkeley High. And I felt it might help matters that we had somewhat similar backgrounds.

When I reported to Scottsdale, Billy told us, "Charlie says he'll be happy if we finish third this year. If anyone's content with third, you can leave now because there's only one place to be. And that's number one!"

So I worked my ass off in Spring Training and was playing some of the best baseball of my life. Billy broke my heart when he told some of the guys that "no faggot's going to ever play on my ball club," obviously referring to me. Billy, evidently, had found out my secret.

I would just never get a chance in the macho game of baseball.

I understood and accepted the reality of it all. So it wasn't hard retiring the second and last time. I was more ready than even the first time. I was relieved. Of course, I still had a choice. Either keep trying to stay in the game, faking who I was, and continue making money, or get on with who I truly was. I didn't know what I would do for work. But I had been able to put some money away from my ball playing. I figured I would amount to little more than a freak. But at least this freak, me, Glenn Burke, was finally going to be able to live his own life! I'd never have to look over my shoulder again!

GROWING UP IN OAKLAND

C omedian. Jock. Protector. I was all of those things growing up in the Oakland elementary school system during the early sixties. Even though my grades were never really too great, I learned a lot about becoming a mature person at a young age. I just learned how to respect people and try to make them smile.

The most important thing I liked about school were the kids. While in class, I'd love to make the other children laugh and feel good. I'd just tell a few jokes and take it upon myself to be the class comedian. Of course, I'd end up almost getting myself kicked out of class my share of times too. But I never tried to be a clown about it. I knew I could only push my act so far.

Despite the normal problems that practically every kid goes through, I was able to kid or joke mine away. I just formed a sense of humor before most of my classmates. And I took pride in having my own language with my own sayings. One of my original favorites that would crack my friends up would occur whenever I saw some frightening-looking dude. I'd say, "He's so ugly, he could scare a hungry bulldog off the back of a meat truck!"

That would usually put them in stitches.

We had a word back in seventh grade called "hoorah."

"Hoorah" was a term for a comedian. The funniest kids would compete to see who the top hoorah was on a given day. For example, the two competing hoorahs would talk about one another in each other's presence while the other kids watching would decide who the best hoorah was based on three determining factors. The first was which one was talking about the other person the most. The second, who was captivating all the attention. And the third was who had earned the circle's approval by the other kids' laughter. Well, many of those kids, including one of the other hoorahs, Vince Trahan, would refer to me as the "first Richard Pryor." They cited this because I could be both funny and verbally dominating. So in the game of hoorah, I was king!

But like I said, I always knew never to cross that line. Whether that be with teachers, coaches, or even my mother. It didn't matter. But going to class was always pretty fun.

Sports, not surprisingly, was a tremendous part of my young life. I was the best athlete in my group. I played jump rope, basketball, softball, football, you name it. I played them all in school. But just as important as playing the sports was listening to my coaches. I had always listened to adults, because I knew as early as age twelve that in order for me to succeed on a particular team, I had to get along with management, regardless of what I had accomplished. So my objectives were to first make the team and, second, to get along with the coach and my teammates. I avoided fights at all costs so I wouldn't get suspended, and worked extra hard to keep my grades up so I wouldn't embarrass myself and get kicked off the team. I was a little kid with all these thoughts running through my head. I would keep thinking to myself, "If Glenn Burke is going to do anything, it's going to be to try and be the best person he can."

And I've found that people don't forget that. When my school friends found out about my current condition, they all came by to see how I was making out. After they read some of the articles that have been circulating about me in the papers, they've all been here. For some, it's been twenty-five years since they last saw me. Every last one I'd ever want to see if I was dying, they've all been here. They're the ones that are giving me the strength. It's so beautiful.

Most twelve-year-olds have athletes they idolize. Not me. The main reason was because I couldn't really watch sports on television. In those days, most sporting events like baseball were played during the day. So my mother, Alice, always had the soap operas on. But that probably helped me become a better ballplayer because, instead of watching TV, I'd be outside playing with the other kids. Come six o'clock, however, I was in that house. My mother was a single parent and had to be strong with each of her eight kids.

Whether my sports were organized, such as in Little League,

or unorganized, as was played on the playground, I loved to compete. And while most kids picked a sport and excelled as best as they could in it, I was rare in that I was a two-sport star, in basketball and baseball. And that was well before anyone ever heard of Bo Jackson or Deion Sanders. There wasn't even that two-sport association back in those days.

Basketball was the sport that was then most recognized for being the most popular among Bay Area "magic" athletes, the superstars. It was the most dominating game. In fact, even though the Kansas City A's moved to Oakland in the late sixties, basketball was more popular than baseball for us all. Maybe it was because in basketball, an athlete can play more "freestyle" than in baseball. In basketball, I could show off my hang-time when putting the ball in the hole! And when one of the brothers would ask me how I could stay up in the air so long, I'd tell them, "Potatoes. Eating potatoes gives me hang-time!"

I don't know if the state of Idaho benefited from my telling the other kids that, but it certainly must have helped their potato sales efforts at Berkeley!

Whereas basketball when I was a youngster was played mostly in unorganized pickup games, baseball was organized by the Oakland Little League. Back in those days, they had the fucking money to put together a great league for us. We had Little League for kids ages nine to twelve, Pony League for thirteen- and fourteen-year-olds, and Colt League for fifteen- and sixteen-year-olds. They still have the leagues for the kids today, but the money goes into so many administrations. They hardly have money for decent uniforms. The quality just isn't the same as it was twenty-five and thirty years ago.

I may have been in the Berkeley school system, but as far as the little leagues went, I played in Oakland. I lived on 62nd Street, which bordered the Berkeley/Oakland line. So even though I played on a regular basis with the Berkeley athletes on the playground, I played with a whole different set of kids from Oakland.

I grew to about five-ten, 180 pounds by age fifteen. I was easily the strongest kid in the Colt League. My crowning moment was hitting a ball measured at five hundred feet, way out of Bushrod Park. That motherfucker was hit all the way up to Telegraph Road. I had the body of a man already and scared the shit out of most of the other kids. But despite all the muscle, I have never to this day lifted weights. Never! And I'm glad I never started. Look what happens to today's ballplayers. Jose Canseco's so musclebound, it's possible for him to pull a muscle by just checking his swing! Even the pitchers are pulling muscles. It's gotten out of hand. I was lucky. God blessed me with the monkey body!

Throughout the little leagues, I had three nicknames. "Mr. Monkey," "Magilla Gorilla," and "Gorilla." I just looked like a fucking monkey in those days. But I also had those big old monkey hands, so people knew I was hung like a fucking gorilla too! Another buddy of mine from Berkeley, Jan James, coined the monkey label on me when I hit a rocket out of San Pablo Park. He stood up and screamed, "Oh, Mr. Monkey, you sure raised a whole lots of hell!"

You had to hear the way Jan yelled that out to fully appreciate it. So every time I'd hit the shit out of a ball, Jan would yell out that phrase in honor of my blast.

Out in the field, I always played either right or center field. I liked using my cannon arm to throw people out. Once during an all-star game at Cal Berkeley, in Diamond Stadium, I played a ball one bounce off the center-field wall and threw a guy out who was trying to score from second. I threw that ball one bounce into the catcher's mitt from 380 feet away. After the runner was called out, I just glared at him. I wasn't showing off by throwing over the cutoff. We would never have gotten him out if I had hit the cutoff. When I was a teenager, I could just dominate in baseball.

I continued playing in the Colt League while I also got involved in high school baseball and basketball. I wanted to play football, but my mother wouldn't allow it. She said I was already involved with too many activities, and she wanted me to work on keeping my grades up. So naturally, I did what my mother said.

More and more kids today show a lack of respect for their parents or guardians than used to. That's wrong. My mother had to raise eight kids practically all by herself. My father left us when I was only eleven months old. He would come around now and again, but I never had the father figure that a lot of the other kids had on a regular basis. My father was kind of hard on me. And he never gave me as much money as my sisters. But at least he'd take me out to the park to play ball once in a while. I could never figure out why he treated me so differently than the girls.

Maybe he just wanted me to be stronger within myself. So I had to deal with his picking on me. We would just butt heads because he wanted me to be hard, kind of like him. But I never wanted to be hard. It wasn't in my plans. I just wanted to have peaceful thoughts all the time. And there's nothing wrong with that. If I see someone crying, I stop and ask them, "What's wrong?" Even if that person's a stranger. I was all over Oakland, everywhere, just trying to make those I came in contact with happier.

I never had anyone to take that male role in my house, but one of my playground basketball buddies, Michael Hammock, came close. Hammock was a little older than I was and lived in the Bushrod area. That guy was a scoring machine! He played guard and was a little bigger than me, and we'd play ball and talk about life for hours at a time. Hammock is now the sports coordinator for the Oakland parks and recreation department. Michael was responsible for getting me involved in a lot of Bushrod Park hoop games when I was the youngest in the group. He believed in me when I needed it most.

As a result, I grew up to return the favor to a lot of other kids who needed looking out for and protection from other people. Before starting pickup games on the court, we would have to choose sides from usually among fifteen kids. Inevitably, thirteen had talent and two were like, "Where the fuck did they come from?" I would always make sure those two kids that didn't have any skills were on my team. No one would ever be left out if they wanted to play on my court. I would protect those kids.

It seemed like I was still protecting kids even into my young adulthood. The best example of my saving a kid's ass was the year after I got out of high school in 1971. I had gone to see a Berkeley High basketball play-off game in Richmond, which has never been the greatest of areas. Berkeley had just beaten Kennedy High to win the TLC (Tournament of Champions). The Berkeley players and their coach, Spike Hensley, went to the parking lot afterward to find that their bus had been stolen. Hensley, who must have been insane at that moment, told his team they would take the bus back with the Kennedy players. It was poor judgment because Berkeley had, after all, just eliminated Kennedy for the season.

And the Kennedy players were pretty pissed about it.

Almost immediately after Berkeley boarded the bus, I noticed the vehicle was shaking like crazy back and forth. Berkeley had some strong guys, like Vince Trahan, future baseball star Rupert Jones, and future NBA veteran John Lambert. But because Lambert, a big white center, was Berkeley's best player, a group of the Kennedy guys started kicking his ass so he wouldn't be able to play against Richmond the next night.

So I ran to the bus, and as I was getting on, everything became silent. I don't mean to brag, but it was as if I had parted the Red Sea. The Kennedy dudes, who were wearing Lambert's and this other smaller kid's ass out, stopped fighting with them. I walked to the back of the bus, where the smaller guy was wedged in a seat, and said to him, "C'mon, let's go sit up front."

The satisfaction I got from saving their asses was great, but

I got even more from watching the fear being drained from the smaller kid's face. He had been saved by Mr. Monkey!

No one ever had to protect me, although my sisters tried to anyway. There were so many of them. I just had an army of sisters looking out for me. Lutha, Joyce, Beverly, and Elona. And they were big girls too! They were some of California's top track stars in high school. But more than their help in protecting me against the elements, they influenced me in the "growing up" department. We never had the sibling rivalries that other families have.

Religion probably contributed a great deal to our family bliss and my wanting to always protect other kids that needed it. I realized at a young age that if I wanted to go to heaven and be like the Lord, I had to let people be themselves and not make them the way I thought they should be. Only the Lord can judge people.

The Lord was my best friend growing up. I mean it. I had a lot of friends, but He was the most important to me. Whenever something went wrong, I'd look up to Him and say, "Oh Lord, help me."

I'd talk to Him for a few minutes and I would tell Him my problems because the Lord was the only one that could do something about them.

Church was the greatest! I attended Ebenezer Church off Ashley Street. I was in both the senior and junior choir. And when I was a youngster, I sang at the "Limelight" in my elementary school. We made an album with our group's picture on it. The name of the record was *Through Children's Eyes*. We sang folk songs and stuff like that. My mother still has that album after all these years.

Another thing about being a Christian really sticks out. California has always had its share of racial problems, especially between the blacks and the whites. I've always believed that we're *all* God's children and should work to get along. I was never color-conscious. I was never prejudiced against anyone. Maybe if more people followed Christ's Word, we could have a kind of heaven on earth. Wouldn't that be beautiful?

You know, a lot of people, even Christians, believe that God hates gay people. They're wrong. I know a lot of homosexuals that are better people and Christians than straight followers. God loves us all. Besides, even science today tells us that gays are born gay. I don't think anyone chooses to be a homosexual. So the Lord isn't going to hate anyone that was born differently from the remaining 90 percent of the population that's straight. It just doesn't work that way.

I never knew I was gay growing up. I didn't truly know I was a homosexual until I was twenty-three. I was always busy with my sports. That's usually how I got out of dating girls throughout school. Playing sports, particularly basketball, really helped.

I may have gone on to play major-league baseball with the Dodgers and the A's, but basketball was always my first choice. I may have been a midget compared to the height of other basketball players, but I was good enough to be named High School Basketball Player of the Year for Northern California in 1970. My greatest attribute was my jumping ability. At only six-one, I was still grabbing an average of eleven rebounds a game. I could jump up there and touch the top of the white square above the basket on the backboard. Dunking was never a problem. Opponents hated me. As I drove down the line on a fast break, I'd be thinking, "I'm scoring. Nobody's gonna stop me. I'm getting my two points!"

The *Oakland Tribune* was always covering the Berkeley games, and one of their columnists labeled me "Baby Elgin," after the great Elgin Baylor. Elgin and I both had that "hang-time." People would say Elgin could stand in the air for four seconds. I had some of his moves, so the *Tribune* called me Baby Elgin.

One of my most lethal moves down the lane was kind of like that famous one that Michael Jordan pulled on A. C. Green during the NBA Championship four years ago. You see it on every Jordan highlight tape. It's the move where he drives to the hole, jumps, and, while in midair, switches the ball from his right to his left hand. A lot of people think Michael created that move. But I was doing that shit way back then. And Jordan's got five or six inches on me.

But 1970 wasn't just a great year for me, it was a great year for our Berkeley team. Our other starters, John Lambert, Dan Palley, Larry Green, and Marvin Buckley, all did an outstanding job that season. We went undefeated and shared the State Championship with Helix High School. Helix was located in Southern California and featured future superstar Bill Walton as their center. They were also undefeated. We could never play them for an undisputed state title because there was no state tournament back then as there is now. But if there had been a tournament of some kind, we would have beaten Helix. We would have had Walton talking to himself. We were that good. What made us so good was our approach to the game. We played a team game, even though a couple of us could have dominated other teams on our own.

There's a trend in the last ten or fifteen years that's changed the NBA, as well. Back in the seventies, I feel athletes were better all-around players. The stars then wouldn't just be great on offense, they would be great on defense too. You would never see any one-dimensional players back then. Now, if a guy scores thirty points a game, no one blinks if he can't play good defense. But what good is scoring all those points if you're giving them right back on the other end of the court?

It may seem from my recollections of my basketball days that I never had an off game. As much as I'd like to say I never did, that's not true. Following graduation, I played in a high school championship game between the Northern California High School Stars and the Southern California High School Stars. It was called the CIF, kind of like an all-star tournament, which was played at the Oakland Coliseum, where the Golden State Warriors play. Keith Wilkes, who would go on to star at UCLA in their John Wooden championship years, was assigned to guard me. Man, was Wilkes tough that day. He scored something like twenty-two points to my eleven. That game still bothers me a little bit. I've often told my friends, "If only I could play that game over, I'd . . ."

My only consolation was in knowing that I was named to the CIF All-Tournament team.

I would always spot college and pro scouts sitting in the stands at our Berkeley games. But times were different back in the late sixties and early seventies. Academics were more important than they are today in playing for a big-time college. They had strict standards, which they'd follow to the letter. Most colleges generally didn't travel all over the country on a regular basis. And their players wouldn't make Nike commercials. But even still, I did get scholarship offers to play at the University of Denver and the University of Nevada. I actually went to Denver to play in 1970, but left after a few months. I just didn't like the climate. It was too cold. So I came home and went to Merritt Junior College for a year.

As for my professional dreams of playing basketball, Al Adels, who's a former coach of the Warriors and now their assistant general manager, talked seriously with me several times about coming to their training camp for tryouts. I thought seriously about what Adels had said, but before their camp opened that year, I was signed by the Dodgers, who had sent a scout named Ray Perry to watch me man center field at Merritt. My joy that I shared with Perry quickly turned to horror. The very next day after signing me, he tragically had a heart attack while driving and hit a telephone pole, which killed him instantly. I felt awful for the guy. My mother and I really thought a lot of him as a person. I'll never forget his patience getting me to sign. Let me explain. I was a nineteen-year-old

San Francisco Giants fan. I, like many Bay Area fans, hated the Dodgers more than any other team in professional sports. I figured if I was going to play professional baseball, it was going to be with the Giants.

In fact, when one of my sisters came down to the recreation center where I was shooting hoops to tell me a scout from the Dodgers was at our house to talk with me, I told her, "I don't want to play for the Dodgers. Leave me alone."

But my sister came back again, this time saying, "If you don't come home, Momma's gonna come here and get you!"

Still, I responded with "I don't care. I ain't playing with no Dodgers. I don't like the Dodgers."

I remember thinking at the time how a bunch of us kids would go to Candlestick Park to watch Willie Mays, Willie McCovey, Juan Marichal, and the rest of the Giants. We'd sit way up top of the upper deck, so high up we could hardly see anything that was happening on the field. But we didn't mind. We'd pack a big lunch and just eat.

So I wanted to hold out for the Giants to come calling for me.

But I never had a chance. My sister came back again, this time with my mother right behind her, so I wised up in a hurry and went back to the house with them. Some of my coaches were there to encourage me into accepting Perry's offer to play in the Dodger organization. And in the back of my mind, I realized that being a black kid from Oakland wasn't all that great. I mean, by turning down the Dodgers, I could get labeled as a black with a bad attitude. My professional sports aspirations had hit a crossroads. There were two potential directions.

But it was the Dodgers, and not the Warriors, who handed me that $5,000 signing bonus. My mother, to say the least, encouraged me to take the Dodgers' offer. So I did.

And that's where my dreams of playing in the NBA died.

I certainly wasn't the only kid out of Berkeley High to have dreams of playing in the NBA. Besides Lambert, another friend of mine, the great Phil Chenier, also came out of my school. Phil made it really big in the NBA. He and I had some wonderful battles on the court. Don't get me wrong, Phil was outstanding; but I could get him so pissed during hoops that his nostrils would flare like a fucking horse! We never played an organized game, only pickups. Chenier graduated from Berkeley in 1968, two years before me.

On the baseball side, the East Bay also developed a fine fraternity. Claudell Washington didn't play high school ball at Berkeley, only Connie Mack, but he went on to have a great career with several teams, including the A's, where he hit .571 for them in their 1974 World Series triumph over the Dodgers. I always liked Claudell. We always had a friendly relationship.

Rupert Jones, besides being a great basketball player at Berkeley, also excelled in baseball enough to have a good major-league career. Rupert was a freshman when I was a senior. He was the expansion Seattle Mariners' very first star. For a few years with the Mariners and then with the Yankees, he was one of the best all-around players in the game. He could steal bases and hit for pretty good power. In fact, when he became a Yankee in 1980, the papers in New York began calling him "Little Reggie," after Reggie Jackson. Those two even shared the same initials!

Like Rupert, another Berkeley homeboy, Al Woods, benefited from major-league expansion in 1977 and became one of the first stars of the Toronto Blue Jays. He'd go on to hit .271 over a seven-year career with the Blue Jays and the Minnesota Twins. Al and I were only a year a part. He was a junior when I graduated.

One of the great things about the Berkeley athletes was how we all kept in touch with one another and invited our homeboys into our professional lifestyle. Rupert, Claudell, Al, and I were always leaving tickets for our friends at the gate to come see us play. And then after games, we'd party with our friends. Our fun was genuine, not like the people that just want to be with you because you're an athlete. One of my best friends both during my playing days and now is Vince Trahan. Nobody enjoyed the professional lifestyle more than him. But it was no problem. He hung with all of the Berkeley athletes when we were playing either at Anaheim or Dodger Stadium. Vince was living in Riverside then, and he'd drive around in that BMW of his and party with some of the players.

But what made Vince especially proper was how he found out I was gay and how he accepted it. Vince was waiting for me in the Dodger Stadium parking lot after a game, dressed to impress. Two of the finest-looking ladies he had ever seen came up to him and asked, "You're one of the players, right?"

Vince said, "I can't lie to you girls, I'm actually a friend of Glenn Burke's."

They got really excited. "Oh, you know Glenn?"

Vince responded by exclaiming, "Oh baby, I went to grade school with Glenn! He's my partner!"

They then asked if Vince was alone. After he said that he was alone, they asked if they could wait with him.

Vince's dick must have been getting hard, because he said, "Oh shit! Hell yeah you can wait with me!"

So they went back into his BMW and smoked a little weed while they waited for me. But after a while, after all the players had pretty much left, the girls must have thought poor Vince was faking the fact that he really knew me. After about a half an hour, the girls left.

The next time he came to a Dodger game I, again, didn't come out. Vince began taking it personally. I must have made him feel more like a groupie than a good friend.

Vince decided to go to one more game, to give me another chance in not blowing him off. While sitting in the stands, some of my gay friends, who I had also left tickets for, overheard Vince talking about me and introduced themselves to him. A friend Vince had taken to the game turned to him and said, "Damn, these motherfuckers are homosexuals!"

But Vince began talking with them anyway. And, as it turned out, they were a big help to him in leading him to where I came out after the game. I was intentionally coming out of the stadium on the other side of the parking lot to avoid all the admiring women. So after that game, Vince was there waiting along with my gay friends, and I felt it was time to let him know my deal. He handled the news so well that he even made an effort to hang out with my new circle of friends.

On one hand, Vince was happy that I filled him in. He knew that none of our other friends knew and was touched I could confide in him with my secret. But on the other hand, he would probably miss the opportunities with the ladies that Rupert and Claudell would help bring him into. I'm not saying Vince needed any help in getting the girls, but being friends with ballplayers could sometimes provide that final stamp needed to close the deal!

There may also be a hint of professional jealousy in people like Vince. I mean, Vince was a great high school athlete who, if things had turned his way a little bit, might have made the big time. But that professional jealousy never got in the way of our friendship these past thirty years. And I don't feel badly for people like Vince, either. They're usually the type that land on their feet. And Vince is no exception. He's been a success in business for years.

Growing up in Northern California was one of the most enriching experiences in my life. It helped shape me into a caring person who loves to make others laugh. I treasure the friends I made here. Because the friends who were with me twenty-five years ago when I was starring at Berkeley are the same ones who have come by to see me in my present ailing state.

They are all true friends.

5

THE "FIRST" GAY MAJOR LEAGUER

Bryant Gumbel had never been more flustered. I had just gone public with my homosexuality in 1982, through a magazine article, and Bryant was interviewing me on the *Today* show. We talked about my being the first major leaguer to ever come out and confirm his homosexuality and how difficult it was being a gay professional athlete. As the interview was coming to a close, I presented Bryant with a Pendulum Pirates' softball cap. The Pendulum Pirates was the name of the gay softball team I was playing for at the time. Bryant didn't know what to say. He was actually speechless!

The guys at the Pendulum Club, the team's sponsor, were ecstatic! They threw a big party for me the next time I went in there. The party wasn't just for giving the Pendulum Club national notoriety. It was also for striking a chord for the gay movement. There I was, on national television, a gay man talking about his baseball career. It was unprecedented.

I had met Gumbel before. He used to be a sportswriter in Los Angeles before moving on to network television news and sports. I always liked and respected Bryant for all he had accomplished. Despite some of the negative press he's received throughout the years in regards to his family life, I admire the fact he was one of the first high-profile black journalists. And I remember him when he was just starting out.

The magazine article that I had made my sexual orientation public through was named, appropriately enough, "The Double Life of a Gay Dodger," and went to print for the October 1982 edition of *Inside Sports*. It was written by the man I had been lovers with for six years, Michael J. Smith.

Michael was always so political about everything and had wanted me to come out since my days with the Dodgers. I never wanted to make my orientation public for several reasons. And I still really didn't give Michael permission to write the article about me in 1982. He did it anyway.

Michael had reasons for writing that article that went beyond politics. He had a huge ego and wanted to get the publicity that such a news item would bring him. He also thought that if he wrote the piece, I'd move back in with him. We had been living apart at the time. And he also did it for the money, which was pretty substantial for a feature like this one in those days. I never did see any of that money. Michael kept it all.

I felt the article was written extremely well. However, there were things in there that I never would have permitted him to write. Things that were personal and very embarrassing. But even though we were on-again, off-again lovers at the time, he never showed me what he had written before he submitted it to *Inside Sports*.

There were several items in the article that were particularly humiliating. Not to mention untrue.

The article stated that I was naive to the gay culture in the Castro as a child growing up in Oakland. That's not true. I knew it existed. I knew there was a place for gays. How did Michael think I found the Castro in 1975? Shit, the place is only a twenty-minute drive from Berkeley.

He also wrote that shit that Mike Norris, my A's roommate, allegedly told him. Michael wrote that Norris said he was nervous around me knowing I was gay. That he would stay out of our room at night until midnight and then worry that I would make a move on him. That the entire A's team was watching out for me. It's bullshit. No one knew about my sexual preferences. Hardly any of those guys were around for more than a cup of coffee with how Charlie was running the club. And even if Norris had known I was gay, he was smart enough to know I never would have made a move on him. I mean, that's ridiculous. A gay man making a move on a straight man is just plain stupid. I just can't imagine Norris saying any of that bullshit.

And the last major problem I had with the article was

Michael quoting me as saying, "I didn't know if I could be gay without being a sissy."

He had to have been kidding with that one. I had seventeen-inch biceps and loved the fact I was built like a fucking tank. I couldn't be a sissy if I wanted to. Not even in my wildest dreams. I knew that from the first moment I came out. Homosexuals come in all shapes and sizes. I've always accepted that fact.

But now, almost thirteen years since Michael wrote that article, I figure if the article helped the gay movement even a little bit, it wasn't such a bad thing. And I think it probably did help.

In a city like San Francisco, there's a lot of gay politics that goes on. And some people have their own agenda. Michael was one of those people. Michael probably "used" me on this project a little bit. But again, if the final result helped the movement, I'm glad I was a part of it.

America, in general, puts a great deal of emphasis on living the straight and narrow lifestyle. Just check out the commercials during a football game. It's just a steady stream of motherfuckers guzzling beer and chasing women. A great part of society still doesn't know how to deal with homosexuality. And there is no sport that accepts gays less than baseball.

There are currently gays in baseball. Just as I wasn't close to being the only homosexual when I was playing ball. And some of those contemporaries of mine were superstars. I won't name them specifically, because I'm not into "outing" dudes, but people would be very surprised.

Gay players live a double life to survive in baseball. But at least they know exactly where they're coming from. To me, it wasn't always hell living the double life. It could actually be kind of fun in certain situations. No one knew where I was coming from. I'd walk through the locker room like a real macho man. And after the Dodgers, A's, and the rest of baseball found out I was gay, they'd say, "Glenn Burke?!"

It threw them for a loop. It had to. And some of them might have looked in the mirror and thought, "Shit, I could be gay, too."

You wake up one morning, like I did, and realize that you could be gay. Trust me. That's how it happens.

So sometimes it takes a foreigner like Martina Navratilova to make Americans think logically about the whole situation.

Since I came out in '82, no other player has claimed to be homosexual. Although longtime National League umpire Dave Pallone came out with a book not long ago called *Behind the Mask*, which went into great detail about how all of those fucking suits with Major League Baseball blackballed him too. And he wasn't even a fucking player! Is it any wonder gays stay in the closet in baseball?

Football seems to be a little more open about homosexuality than baseball, but not by much.

Dave Kopay, the former running back with the 49ers and the Redskins, once wrote a book on his homosexuality. I think it became a best seller. He was the first football player to come out. Years later, a few of the San Diego Chargers came out too.

Those Chargers, I don't believe, were ever really named in the press. But Kopay was different. He came all the way the fuck out.

I got to meet Kopay during my playing days. We compared notes. He told me he overcompensated his aggression on the field to hide his homosexuality from the football world. Because football is a contact sport, that overcompensating wasn't a hard thing for him to accomplish.

But baseball's different. In baseball, you have to be more relaxed. You have to be able to concentrate on a pitch coming at you ninety miles per hour.

I explained that dilemma to Kopay, and he just recommended I go by my instincts. Which I did, but I suppose not well enough.

If you're a football player and gay, it's much easier to stay single. Nobody's going to question you because you're usually so fucking big. But in baseball, there's nobody to talk to about the subject. A big percentage of the gays I knew and knew of in baseball got married to women they didn't love. They did it just to save face. Like what the Dodgers wanted me to do.

So why do gay athletes in America stay in the closet? Because it can be an awfully cruel and unfair world outside of it.

6

LIFE IN THE CASTRO

Castro Street in San Francisco has a higher percentage of homosexuals than any other corner of the world. If there was a planet for gays, the Castro would be it. The entire social strata, from the doctors, lawyers, and politicians down to the gas station attendants and shoe shiners, everyone is homosexual. The Castro is situated off of one of the most scenic strips of roadway in all of California. Less than a mile from 18th Street and Castro is Potrero Hill, which overlooks the San Francisco Bay. Not far in the other direction is Russian Hill, which overlooks Fisherman's Wharf. On a clear California afternoon, the views are breathtaking.

The Castro is still beautiful, but it's not as wonderful as it was in the seventies and eighties. It used to be the place to be. Even after the bars would close at night, people would just hang on the street, socialize, and have a great time. There was hardly ever any trouble. Now, however, it's a little dirtier, with a lot of runaways, homeless people, and drug problems.

Yet the Castro still has a sense of community. Tens of thousands live in the Castro, yet everybody seems to know everybody else. As a child, I knew of the Castro. Little did I know that I would realize my own homosexuality and one day live in this community.

One of the great things about living among all gay people is the safety-in-numbers aspect. Only once do I recall any real trouble from gay-bashers, who were in full force ten and fifteen years ago. It occurred just off the strip when a group of hecklers were getting on this queen they didn't even know. I stepped in and was able to intimidate those assholes enough so that they backed off. But that was the extent of any trouble from outsiders.

Once in a great while, as in any other part of society, there would be violence within the gay community. The owner of one of my favorite hangouts, Uncle Bert's, was murdered in 1984 when a young "hustler" stabbed him fourteen times. The victim, Everett Hedrick, was able to crawl himself to a bus stop to give the hustler's description to the police over the phone before dying. A suspect was arrested later that night.

Hustlers can be very different from one another. Some hustle for money, others for a place to stay, and some for nothing more than to prove to themselves they're not straight. Then there are "straight hustlers" who are looking for nothing more than trouble, preying mostly on older white men and blacks.

Another night at Uncle Bert's, Everett was arrested in his own bar. He was a great man when sober, but on this one night he got drunk and the racist side of him came out. He kicked all the blacks out of the place before my good friend Jack McGowan called the police. Jack was always standing up for what was right.

I liked Uncle Bert's over some of the other bars for several reasons. First of all, it was one of the first gay "sports bars," which featured free drinks whenever the 49ers scored a touchdown. In addition, I played for their softball team for a couple of years, and the place had a patio in the back where I could hang out in the fresh air. I don't smoke, and a lot of times people smoke in bars. It gets all over your clothes and up in your lungs. I was, and still am, into staying clean and healthy.

The place I first spent most of my time at was the Pendulum. McGowan helped run the place and got me involved with their softball team. In the late seventies, it was presumed to be a hangout, but it really wasn't. The owner, Rod Kobila, was one of the greatest sponsors gay softball has ever had. But then in the late eighties the Pendulum became a dark, loud, and boisterous all-black bar. It can actually be pretty dangerous in there at times. Plus, I got burned out there. Every time I was on the street, someone would ask, "What time are you headed for the Pendulum?"

So I stopped going there, and began going to other places

like Bad Lands, Castro Station, Sutter's Mill, and, of course, Uncle Bert's.

I really first discovered the benefits of the Castro following my season at Waterbury in 1975. I would, at first, just visit the area and go to the bars. Then, I began to make friends. Some of them became friends that I still have today. And I would end up staying with some of those friends for days at a time. It was such a relief to have the support and friendship of these great people.

A couple of months or so into that off-season, before heading to Albuquerque, a happening occurred that altered my life forever. At a bar on Fulsom Street, I met Michael Smith. Michael was about six-two, slim, had dark hair but light skin. He had very chiseled, handsome features, a cross between Gary Cooper and Gregory Peck. Michael was also extremely intelligent. He graduated Harvard with a 4.0, with concentrations in Music and Public Speaking. Michael was also very political. He would later become one of the founders of "the Quilt," which was sewn in remembrance of all those who have died of AIDS. And true to my personal preference, he was about ten years older than me. In a word, I was in awe of him.

Little did I realize at the time that I would spend six years living with this man as his lover.

Michael's reasons for being attracted to me were simpler. At age twenty-three, I had a fabulous body. I had enormous shoulders and a rippled chest. My waist was very thin, while my legs, thighs, and arms were very big and muscular. I was a showpiece for him.

We fell in love with each other, and before long I moved in with him. It would be the beginning of a roller coaster–like relationship. When we weren't in love, we were fighting. And since he taught Public Speaking at the time, it was hard to argue with him. So I'd just end up going downstairs and shutting the door or visiting with my friend "B.W.," who lived up on Hill Street, about five blocks away from 18th and Castro.

The problem was, one minute Michael would make me feel like the most wonderful person in the world, then he would turn on me and become very critical and vicious. He had a power of control over me. Michael could also be a snob. Because he was so intellectual, he would mock my "lack of intelligence" in the presence of my friends. For instance, he would always joke with our friends about how he could never get me to go to the opera with him. He made me feel like I was just another one of his projects. Like in *My Fair Lady*, he was trying to make me something I wasn't. And this wouldn't just piss me off, it would piss off my friends too. They never let any kind of education or their exposure to life ever interfere with friendships. They didn't care how smart I was. It had nothing to do with anything. It didn't matter. My friends saw a different side of me than Michael did. We never used each other like Michael did with me time and time again. We instead would take turns buying each other dinner and drinks and we'd even exchange Christmas presents during the holidays. We were true friends in every way. I never truly felt that with Michael.

After I moved in with Michael, his apartment suddenly became "party central." We had several parties or gatherings a week with our friends in that place. The parties were fun. We'd have some of his friends, some of mine. A real wide range of characters.

His friends, of course, were much different than mine. One of Michael's best friends at the time was an organist from a college in San Rafael. With Mike being a music major, they always had a strong bond in that respect. Michael would often play piano during our parties. Although he truly played an excellent piano, he did it to draw attention to himself.

Another friend of Michael's was into meditation. So we had a meditation party with about ten of our friends. His friends loved it. Mine could hardly wait to leave. But Michael prolonged the "party" by giving a lecture discussing our mantras. The speech, along with his making a fool of me at times, didn't exactly endear him to my friends.

With the exception of McGowan, my buddies never really interfered in my relationship with Michael. I guess they felt it would just make matters worse for me. But I could tell how they felt. I recall so many days when I would walk someplace in the Castro and people would shout to me from a block away, "Hey Glenn, what's going on? What's happening?!"

And I would shout hello back, smiling and joking around. However, when I was walking with Michael around town, people stayed away. The shouts changed to feeble-like comments such as "Hi, Glenn," and nothing more. Others would just walk right on by saying nothing.

Perhaps my closest ally at the time was B.W. Like I said, when things got hot around the household with Michael, I would go and see him. I met B.W. after my season at Waterbury, on a beach in the Bay Area. I was hanging with a guy he knew from the Castro, and that broke the ice in our meeting one another. After spending some time talking at the beach, we went back to B.W.'s apartment for something to eat.

A couple of days later, I saw B.W. again, this time in the Castro while I was with another mutual friend, Wes Jackson, and he invited us up to his apartment to listen to some music and have a few drinks. B.W. was as kind and warm as a person can be. We really developed a good rapport with one another, a positive rapport. But it was never sexual. We were and always have been very close friends. He was like an older brother in that I could always tell him what was on my mind. B.W. is an excellent listener. I could tell him about my baseball playing and how it conflicted with the mainstream macho athlete. I think he found me pretty interesting. The best thing about our friendship, though, was how we could trust each other. Our secret thoughts were safe with one another.

If I ever had a friend who was there for me in good times and bad, it was B.W. He was there for me in probably my lowest point in my professional career. B.W. drove me to the Holiday Inn in Oakland following the 1977 season, for a meeting I was to have with Al Campanis. I had assumed the point of the meeting with Al was to have a positive discussion about renewing my

Dodger contract for 1978 and beyond. I was pumped up about the meeting. I was coming off a good season and was still their top prospect. I felt it was my time to begin moving up the financial ranks of big-league ball. As I left B.W.'s car, I told him I didn't think the meeting would take very long and that he could come in with me if he wanted to. He felt it wouldn't be appropriate and said he'd sit in the parking lot and read the *Chronicle*.

I was on cloud nine as I entered the Holiday Inn. I was practically hopping and skipping, just full of life. But that euphoria would soon change, as this short meeting would end up lasting at least of couple of hours. Al was making his bid with me to find a woman and get married. He also began to make it clear that my career with the Dodgers was in jeopardy if I didn't follow through with his wishes.

So after a good long meeting, I approached B.W.'s car, head hung, and got into the car. I told him, "I'm ready to go now."

He said, "Okay."

B.W. was trying to be helpful, but I told him, "You don't mind if I don't want to talk, do you?"

He said, "Of course. That's fine."

So we drove all the way back to San Francisco without saying a word. He dropped me off at the corner of 18th and Castro, and I caught a bus to go visit a friend and chill out for a while. B.W., who was older and more mature than I was, always tried to help me, but he also knew that at times it helped just as much for him to be with me and not say a word.

B.W. was also there for me in some of my happiest times. Like when I bought that car with my World Series share. That car was as much a symbol of my independence as anything else I had in my life. And because Michael was such a dominant type, my purchase infuriated him. So I called B.W. and told him I was going to pick *him* up today in my new car. We went out to lunch on Castro Street to celebrate and then drove around aimlessly for hours. We then stopped by my apartment to show Michael. It was probably the angriest I've ever seen him.

B.W. was also one of my friends that would attend the parties Michael and I had. He saw Michael as many of my other friends saw him, as a control freak. He saw how everyone had to do things Michael's way or they would be treated with contempt. B.W. knew what I was up against in Michael, a man who his own friends "lovingly" referred to as "The Wicked Witch of the West"!

But never did B.W. put Michael down in front of me. He knew I loved Michael and swallowed much of Michael's berating of people at our parties. B.W., like so many of my other friends in the Castro, was much older than I was. They perhaps had forgotten what it was like to think as a twenty-three-year-old. I put up with the bullshit because Michael was a very handsome man who, when he wanted, could charm a snake.

B.W.'s house was like a buffer for me. I could just chill out there. I actually had my own room! And when I asked B.W. if it would be all right for me to get a bigger bed, not only did he say he didn't have a problem with it, he called a friend of his who had an extra queen-size mattress. And B.W. went to his friend's to pick it up for me, free of charge!

When Michael came over and saw the bed, he turned to B.W. and asked, "What are you trying to do to Glenn and me?"

B.W. responded incredulously, "Me?"

Michael was steamed. "Obviously, you've planned for Glenn to stay here for a long time."

"I had nothing to do with it," B.W. said. "It was Glenn's idea, and all I did was find him a bed."

I was starting to get pissed off at Michael's interrogation. I shouted at Michael, "Look, bud, this is my business! I did this! You have nothing to say to B.W. about this!"

Michael stormed out and that was the end of that.

Maybe I was running away from my problems with Michael by staying at B.W.'s place, but I didn't care. I never liked confrontations. Besides, B.W. would invite his friends over and we would have a great time.

When I would return to Michael, things would progressively get worse over time. He was trying to get me to do things I really didn't want to do. The worst thing was his trying to alienate me from my homeboys from Oakland and Berkeley. Really, he didn't even want me to have Castro friends either. Just his friends.

Predictably, Michael began to despise B.W. He made that

very clear to him. Michael began accusing B.W. of babying me and letting me have my way all the time. He wasn't happy about how easy it was for me to just pack up and leave for B.W.'s house. B.W. and I just ignored him.

I invited Alan out to San Francisco from Connecticut to stay with me at B.W.'s, and Michael went absolutely nuts when he found out. Alan was such a breath of fresh air compared to the abuse I was getting from Michael. I just wanted the companionship. Michael, of course, knew our history together. And not only was Alan competition for Michael in a romantic way, he was a Yale professor. Michael, despite being a Harvard graduate, was only selling real estate. That just added fuel to the fire.

The next thing I knew, Michael had thrown all my shit out on Collingwood Street, where we lived. Not just my clothes, but all my possessions too. That was, needless to say, the end of my first tour of duty with Michael. We had been together at that point for about a year.

I called B.W. immediately and he drove right over. He could see how humiliated I looked and couldn't help me enough. He helped me pick up my things and we loaded up his car. I called my mother and told her she could reach me over at B.W.'s house. I ended up staying at B.W.'s quite a bit over the next two years when I would come into San Francisco. Otherwise, I went home to my mother's in Oakland. Friends don't come any better than B.W.

B.W. and I are still great friends today. He's teaching schoolchildren back east. One of my fondest memories of him was when he'd come to the Oakland Coliseum when I was with the A's. B.W. would sit out there in the bleachers behind me in center field. He would sit right up next to the fence and between hitters would talk to me. In was fun to interact with him while I was playing ball. He was just always there for me. Period.

I was beginning to feel better about things after Michael and I split up. Michael, however, developed a sort of fatal attraction toward me. He became more and more vicious toward my whole circle of friends whenever he'd see them around the Castro. He would also follow me around and make a scene everywhere I went. His only interest was keeping me under his thumb. But this strategy of his, whatever he was out to accomplish by it, failed badly. He'd look like a chump after a while. He'd come into a favorite hangout of mine like Sutter's Mill, which was filled with people who were in business, the theater, or gay softball, and he'd feel like a total outsider. Those types of people were impressed that I played professional baseball, but were equally impressed with my being just a regular kind of guy. They disliked Michael because all he cared about was himself.

Another thing Michael tended to do was to be sure he always had a date who was black whenever he knew I'd probably be around. In fact, Michael only dated black men. But those relationships never lasted more than one or two weeks. He was a user. A destroyer. He had at least a one-nighter with almost every black guy who hung out at the Pendulum. He thought this would make me jealous. And angry. Instead, I would get somewhat depressed over the whole thing. But at the same time, I was flattered by his obsession with me. I was so young!

Eventually, I started seeing Michael again. I guess he was starting to wear me down. Must have been that Ivy League look of his!

I really made a commitment to keeping an open mind with Michael. And to not let him get the best of me. Many times, we were able to get along better than before. But other times, he became a great source of embarrassment. Much of that embarrassment stemmed from him wanting me to come out of the closet during the 1977 World Series, when I was with the Dodgers. I guess he felt it would have been a great thing for the gay cause. Many gays feel that it's perfectly all right to "out" another homosexual to make the general public aware of how gays have filtered into the mainstream of society. I, of course, saw it as baseball suicide.

An example of what Michael was trying to accomplish was displayed during Game 3 at Dodger Stadium. The night began so nicely. We were back at home all tied up with the Yankees at one game apiece, and the fans were going wild for us. Before the game, the public address announcer was introducing the teams as we'd line up along the first- and third-base foul lines.

When they called my name, I noticed Roy Campanella sitting in a wheelchair not far from home plate. Campanella was being honored that night for his lifetime achievements with the Dodgers as both a Hall of Fame catcher and a coach. So instead of jogging right out to join the other Dodgers, I first went over to give Campanella a hug. I didn't do that to draw attention to myself, which I had, because the fans went crazy. I did it because I really respected the hell out of the courage Campanella had displayed all those years. He overcame his career-ending car accident and paralysis to coach from the wheelchair. Amazing!

Once the game started, Michael started up. I had gotten Michael and a group of his friends tickets for the game, and he wasted little time before becoming an asshole. He started yelling shit about our relationship together. It always started with something like, "Glenn and I . . . ," or "I'm doing this for Glenn." The fans were starting to get annoyed, if not a little more than confused.

Finally, my friend Wes Jackson, who was sitting across the aisle from Michael, intervened. Wes walked over and told Michael to shut his mouth. Wes was always a pretty intimidating-looking guy, and, for that night anyway, Michael didn't really say anything else.

The next day, a Saturday afternoon game, I got a bunch of tickets for my friends and for Michael and his father. These were fabulous World Series tickets. They were sitting between home plate and third base. Besides Wes, I invited B.W. and another friend, Bob Linquist. Bob was Wes's partner. And despite all of Michael's shit the night before, along with our loss to the Yankees, I was still in good spirits. My friends and I were all going to meet after the game at Bob's aunt and uncle's place in Sherman Oaks for a buffet. And we would follow that up by going to a dance club in Hollywood later that night.

Michael and his father sat right in front of my friends' seats. His father knew all about his son's relationship with me and didn't seem to flinch when Michael again began shouting shit about him and me. Other fans began turning their heads toward Michael, again in disbelief. I felt as badly for my friends as I felt worried about myself. They must have felt like crawling under their seats. I guess Wes didn't want to make a scene in front of Michael's father, or else he might have kicked his ass right there in Dodger Stadium.

It was probably a stupid thing of me to have done at the time, but I allowed Michael to meet me in the Dodger locker room sometimes after games. But I had a cover for when he'd say something inappropriate. I'd just lead people on to believe he was my agent. To a certain degree, Michael did control me. He got me to do things I just didn't want to do.

Michael's public outbursts didn't stop in the World Series. One of my most embarrassing moments with Michael was after the A's sent me down to the minors in 1980. I was playing a game in San Jose, and after the final out was made, Michael and his entourage ran right down to the dugout as I was jogging off the field. I tried to be polite, but I had no control over the situation. There must have been twenty-five of these faggots, some of whom behaved poorly, running down to see me. None of them cared what I had just been through with Tom Lasorda or Billy Martin. None of them cared that I was trying to get back up to the big leagues. I don't think Michael even knew some of those queens. It seemed like Michael had just pulled a bus up to a corner in the Castro and yelled, "Road trip!"

Besides, Michael never had twenty-five true friends in his whole life. It hurt me badly that he did this to me. It showed he didn't care about my goal of getting back with the A's. He just cared about his own political agenda. Like when he wrote the "Gay Dodger" story in 1982 for *Inside Sports*. If I wasn't out of the closet completely before the article, I was certainly out after it was printed.

The combination of keeping an open mind and Michael's obsession with getting me completely back in his life led to a conversation we had about moving back in with one another. We had been living apart for two years. The talk included the financial advantages of pooling our money together to buy his rented apartment and make it more valuable. He said it would make a great investment for us both when it came time to sell the place. I had just received $65,000 from the A's in severance pay that I had no idea what to do with. So I agreed to move back in with Michael and gave up most of my money to use in refurbishing the apartment, under the assumption that my name would be put on the deed. I trusted Michael a little too much, however, as I would find out years later that he never did add my name.

Once remodeled, I figured our place would instantly become the centerpiece for some of the best parties the Castro would ever see. We put in a skylight and fixed up a fabulous deck in the back. That place was gorgeous. And I really thought Michael and I were going to get along much better because we were now linked financially. So we had our first party once the decorating was completed. For all the changes Michael and I had talked about and done, just as many things remained the same as before. Michael never made my friends feel more uncomfortable. B.W., Wes, Manny, and a few others ended up leaving after maybe fifteen minutes. Michael just hated my friends. He probably would have tried to punch them all out if he could have. So I just accepted Michael in this respect. There would be no more trying to change him. Michael thought he had me under his thumb because of our financial arrangement and continued to try and keep me from my buddies. But he would never change that about me, and he at least began to try and accept that fact.

Eventually, I got tired of all of Michael's shit and left him about four years later. I learned that you can never try and change someone and to never allow anyone to change the things you like about yourself. It was a painful and expensive lesson to learn. Michael would eventually come down with the HIV virus, and he died of AIDS in 1988, about four years after we broke up.

I began to re-devote my life to competitive sports after Michael and I broke up. My two greatest interests were the Gay Men's Softball League and the Gay Olympic Games.

The Gay Men's Softball League became popular in the Bay Area in 1973 when they began having tournaments. My buddy Jack McGowan was the founding father of the league and struggled to get Castro restaurants and bars to sponsor the teams needed to make it all happen. It became so popular in the seventies that the championship teams would have a convertible parade up Market Street. The name of the league was changed from Gay Community Softball to Gay Men's Softball, and it's now the most successful outfit of its kind in the country. There are now thirty-two teams around the United States. San Francisco used to always dominate the league, but now that there is more openness for gays in other cities, every team is on a more even playing field.

In San Francisco, it was and still is a true event. A typical game has male cheerleaders and crowds of about three hundred people. During the play-offs, the games can draw more than fans. And when we play the police force, which includes mostly straights, the crowd can grow in excess of eight thousand rowdy onlookers. The league became so popular that it was not that uncommon for the star players to be wined and dined by groupies. The best players could even make under-the-table deals with their sponsors for money and free drinks. Payoffs like those were often kept hush-hush. It was just so competitive.

I got involved in the league because of Jack, the manager of the Pendulum Pirates. That was in 1981, the year after I left baseball. Along with B.W., Jack is still one of my dearest friends. It's like, when I see him, a fire comes over me. As if the Lord is present. It's like when a person sees someone they treasure, a vibe comes through. A feeling always comes over me with him and I feel like saying something like "Hey Jack, do you want to do something?" or "Do you want to grab a drink? Let's talk for a minute."

Only with Jack, you can never talk for just a minute. He's a real talker. It's tough even for me to get a word in when Jack's talking to me. You just have to tape that "girl's" mouth!

A lot of times, gay people refer to another dude as a girl. Well, in Jack's case at times, it may have been considered appropriate. Appropriate, that is, when he was in the navy. Jack's best friends refer to him as "Irene," because when he was in the navy in 1949, he performed for the boys wearing drag. The name just stuck all these years.

Before "Irene" was my softball coach, I knew him as the head manager of the Pendulum Club. We met while I was playing with the Dodgers, and when he found out who I was, he flipped. You see, Jack is the biggest sports fan I've ever met.

In addition, he's the only writer in the country who covers gay sports. He's worked at the *San Francisco Sentinel,* California's gay and lesbian weekly newspaper, for years. He knows sports trivia better than anyone, so we hit it off extremely well. In fact, on one of his birthdays, I gave him my first Dodger uniform as a gift. The gesture meant the world to him. I had that white jersey cleaned and pressed for him. He's such a nice man. We now sit and cry and talk about a lot of things that are going on in our lives. He's the type of person that speaks truths. And a lot of times gay people don't want to hear the truth. They just want to go out and party and go home with somebody and shit like that. That's all they think about. It's their whole world. Those queens don't have time to listen to real, reasonable things. Things that really matter. Then you get a few of them by themselves and you find out they're all decent people. But when they're out in the public eye, they're just out to have a good time.

If there's a person on the face of this earth I'd want to be friends with, it's Jack "Irene" McGowan!

Another thing I love about Jack is how he helps people. He would end up managing that Pendulum Pirates team of his for fifteen years. But besides being a very dedicated manager, he encouraged his players to do something with their lives besides just hanging out at bars. And they responded for the most part to that encouragement in a positive way. He also formed a very cohesive group that included whites, hispanics, blacks, and orientals. He always had very multiracial teams. And whenever there was a problem within the ranks, he would use his patented phrase, "Oh Dear Heart, take a break." Plus, he knew he could back it up if he had to.

I've been told by those who have followed Gay Men's Softball throughout the years that I was the league's greatest all-time player. That may be so, but Jack often reminds me about his claim to fame when he struck me out three times in a game in Sacramento. It was a work of art. But remember, in softball, a fouled third strike is ruled a strikeout. And that's what happened!

Jack is one of the most competitive people I've ever met outside of professional ball. And he wasn't afraid to show off that competitiveness as a coach. He once brought in a relief pitcher for "Glenda Boom Boom" Black, a tough drag queen who was once an all-American basketball player, while he was pitching a no-hittter through five innings of an all-star game. I guess Jack felt it was the best move for the team. His favorite motto was always "Not winning is not a sin, but not wanting to is."

A real coach's coach!

When I first began in Gay Men's Softball, I was a much better fielder than hitter. I could cover the entire left side of the infield and throw people out from my knees. But when it came to hitting, it took me a while to adjust to that slow pitch shit. I mean, it's difficult in the space of a year to go from a

J.R. Richard one-hundred-mile-an-hour special to a rainbow pitch. But after a while I adjusted and hit the ball wherever I wanted to. Jack would tell me I became so good, guys wouldn't want to join the league because they were afraid of me.

In that first year, 1981, we were the San Francisco League champions and went to Toronto to play in the Gay World Series. Several guys that I'm still close with today, like Jack and Ed Snyder, were associated with that team. Even B.W. worked for the commissioner at the time. It was, perhaps, the happiest year of my life.

I've always had tremendous respect for other athletes. When I would throw out people from my knees, some people who didn't know me perceived that to be me being a showboating "I'm better than you" show-off. But it was never like that. I would do things on occasion if someone playing for the opposition tried to show up my team. I was very supportive of my teammates. I tried to be a leader. And that was whether I was playing center field for the Dodgers or shortstop for the Pendulum Pirates. I tried to approach all levels of sports the same, professional way.

Following the Gay World Series, I was invited to the Cable Car Awards they used to have at the Kabuki Theater in San Francisco. It's a really huge theater where they put on many special events. To my great honor, I was voted by my peers as the Softball Player of the Year and received my award on stage. This wasn't a homosexual award; it was an honor that was given by both gays and straights. People from both "orientations" would get together and compare notes. From those meetings, they would nominate and vote for the best of everything and everyone in San Francisco. It didn't hurt, I suppose, that both Jack and another friend of mine, Bob Gocklindorf, were on the panel. Bob was a captain in the navy at the time. Winning a Cable Car Award was a great accomplishment.

The Gay Softball League has changed a lot since the days when I played. It's much more political because homosexuality is now out in the open. Cities now actually bid on getting the Gay World Series. And players are more tied to their teams now than they were then. I played for several different bars and restaurants in the early eighties. It was perfectly all right to move to whatever team you wanted. It's so much more structured now.

The Gay Olympic Games was a means of getting me involved again with my all-time favorite sport of basketball. The Gay Olympic Games were founded by Tom Waddell, who finished sixth in the 1968 Olympic Decathlon, and by Mark Brown, in 1982. Back then, the Gay Games had no trials. It was all-inclusive and all were welcome to join. At times, it was ridiculous that some out-of-shape gays would come out to compete. Some of them, it seemed, would take thirty minutes to run the hundred-yard dash! But at the very least, it got people together in a healthy, competitive environment.

In those 1982 games, hosted by San Francisco, I played both basketball and baseball. In basketball, I averaged forty points over a six-game span. I was named the MVP of that sport. We had some other great athletes, but I just went all out.

We took the Gay Olympic World Series as well, and the Pendulum Club threw us a huge party after the games were over. The police closed off the side street that the Pendulum is on and just let us have it for the night. Our team knew the police. We beat them to death in an all-star game in the City League. They couldn't fuck with us. We batted around twice. They couldn't even get back up to hit. The umpires had to call the game. And I hit a ball so hard I broke one of the officer's kneecaps. I felt badly about that, but we were going for the "No Mercy Rule." We really wanted to kick their ass. The rout was our way of earning some respect from the police. And all the while, we'd call out to them, "Straight boys, straight boys. We're gonna beat you. Straight boys, straight boys."

Everyone started laughing. We were acting like a bunch of sissies.

But we figured that showing our superiority at softball would help our cause. And somewhere along the line, the gays in the Castro did get some respect out of it. So I like to think my contribution to gays was my accomplishments in sports. Nobody could fuck with us anymore.

When they had the closing ceremonies at the Kezar, where the 49ers used to play, I just couldn't move. I had played so hard that when they called out my name to receive a medal, I was just sprawled out on the field, spread-eagled.

By 1986, when the Gay Olympics were held in New York, you could tell the other cities had become increasingly more liberal about gays. Perhaps as a result, our San Francisco contingent finished third in softball. But it's tough to repeat a championship no matter what scenario it is. In our case, every major city in the country was after our ass.

After my six-year relationship with Michael Smith, I would go on to have two other significant lovers that I went with for a while. And there were other lovers for me during, between, and after those two. You see, gay relationships are different than straight ones in ways other than the obvious. Within gay relationships, there is often a little more variety than what exists in straight ones. There often reaches a point with gays where one of the people involved in a twosome wants a little more freedom. I think this is so because there isn't really anything tying the couple together—like marriage. There just isn't a formal bond. And perhaps for athletes, like myself, the sexual appetite is stronger than for the nonathlete. I had a strong sexual appetite and things were very available to me. But that didn't mean I wasn't discreet about it. Like on the ball field, I never threw anything in anybody's face. If I ever strayed from a relationship, I was doing it to satisfy something within me, never intending it to be harmful or hurtful to anyone else. I've always gone out of my way to never hurt anyone else.

Those two special men in my life included Roy, an engineer at a major air force base, and Stan, an interior decorator from

England. Stan and I actually lived together for a while on Beaver Street. One of my objectives in my Beaver Street home was to pay back some of my friends who helped me during my troubled times with Michael. Especially B.W. I must have invited him over two or three times a week for dinner. And I would always have the latest music for B.W. to listen to. I think I made a pretty good host. My friends, who really looked out for me after my relationship with Michael, basically liked all my other lovers. And that meant a lot to me. It meant that I could combine my time with relations and friends without anyone feeling awkward.

The gay lifestyle, coupled with the fact that it was the late seventies and early eighties—the height of the Sexual Revolution, increased the level of intensity of the acquired immune deficiency syndrome that is now commonly referred to as AIDS. The deadly disease has taken the lives of two hundred or so people that I've known within the past fifteen years. It's been devastation!

Gays have had to adapt. But as a result, gays are no longer leading all other groups in contracting new cases of the disease. Of course, that probably has a lot to do with our group being the first to be hit the hardest by AIDS. Safe sex and the use of condoms have become a part of our mainstream.

One of my best softball buddies, Bob Thomas, was the first of my friends to die of AIDS, in 1982. He opened my eyes to the reality that the as yet unnamed disease, the "gay disease" that they called it then, really existed. Bob just didn't look well one day. He complained of a cold that wouldn't go away and really bad stomach problems. Everything he ate turned to diarrhea. He checked himself into the Pacific Medical Center, and his condition worsened significantly. In a matter of days, Bob was dead.

The AIDS epidemic doesn't just kill those who contract the disease, either. Let me explain. Wes Jackson was one of my dearest friends to die from AIDS. He, Manny Simmons, and I were like brothers. We were all black, gay jocks, and the two of them really helped teach me who I was when I first discovered my homosexuality. When Wes died of AIDS, his roommate and lover of sixteen years, Bob Linquist, struggled to come up with the needed funds to pay for the crippling number of medical bills that are involved with any patient of this disease. Bob had to dissolve the property they had both owned south of San Francisco, but the money from that transaction still wasn't enough. Bob, who worked as a fund-raiser at Stanford University, had acquired a valuable manuscript. Valuable enough, he figured, to sell off in order to pay off the rest of Bob's medical bills. But he couldn't sell it for the amount of money that was still needed. So Bob, soon after burying Wes, committed suicide. He had died both with a broken heart and practically penniless. The moral is, the victims of AIDS include people other than the patients themselves.

I had very little money in 1986. Michael had seen to that by "robbing" me of the money I had put into his apartment. I would work at a health club and do things like that to get by. But drugs were increasingly becoming very easy to get ahold of. I began to fall into a trap. My lover Stan was always offering me pot, and the softball players I began hanging around with were doing a lot of coke. Like in most urban areas, it was just becoming the thing to do.

I never got hooked on it, but just did it more often than I had before because everyone else was doing it too.

The Castro had changed a lot in those ten years. It began as a place where gays could feel safe and free. And ended with heavy drug use and an awareness and fear of AIDS.

7

THE FREE FALL

've always known how lucky I was to have the family I have. But it wasn't until the eighties that I truly learned just how strong our family unit really is. And it was my mother, Alice, who was most responsible for keeping everything together. It must have been an awesome task for her. I mean, that woman went through the coming out of a gay son who later came down with the AIDS virus, a daughter who was murdered, and seeing that same gay son being sent to prison three times. But somehow, we're as strong and as close as a family can be.

Telling my family I was a homosexual was one of the most difficult things I've ever had to do. I think they may have put the pieces together before I revealed my orientation. But not knowing that for sure really put a lot of stress on me. In fact, after my revelation to myself in Connecticut, I didn't go home to see my mother for months. I just couldn't bring myself to do it. But I loved my mother and family so much that eventually I confessed my homosexuality in a very private way. And to my surprise, they didn't trip at all. They didn't say a negative thing about it. They just accepted it.

Afterward, I would bring some homosexual friends over for Thanksgiving and Christmas. These were friends that couldn't make it home to be with their families. I would bring four or five of them over every holiday so they could meet my family. I was so much luckier than 99 percent of the homosexuals out there, most of whom wouldn't dream of bringing another gay person into their family's home for fear they would be made to feel uncomfortable.

My sister Elona was so accepting of my lifestyle that she would come to the funerals of my friends who died of AIDS and put carnations on their caskets. That's an example of the type of person Elona was. Elona was only a year older than me, so we grew up very close to one another. She was such a tomboy, always defending and fighting my battles for me at school. And what an athlete! She was a world-class sprinter in the seventh grade. Berkeley High School would send a driver to pick her up at junior high to take her to the varsity squad events. Her great grades in school helped make that scenario possible.

So when Elona was murdered a little over ten years ago, it was a big blow to the family. She died trying to stop a dispute between two male friends of hers. While playing peacemaker, she got stabbed in the hip. Shocked and scared, she ran into the bathroom and locked herself in. It took the fire department forty minutes to get through the door. She bled to death as a result.

Elona was survived by her husband and five kids. Neither myself nor the family has ever been quite the same. It had a profound effect on us all. But it also brought us all even closer to one another.

It's a comfort to us all, though, to know that girl's in heaven with the Lord.

After Elona's death, I wasn't really involved with anyone in particular. I was living at home with my mother and coming into San Francisco as often as I could. I would crash with a lot of my friends in the Castro, but nothing even remotely permanent. Besides, I liked being back home. My mother is a fabulous woman, and I was kind of representing a much-needed male role model for my little brother Sidney. Sidney was only a teenager then, and he sometimes got himself into a little bit of trouble. Never anything serious, but I enjoyed helping him with schoolwork and talking to him about how to work through everyday problems. Perhaps more than anyone I know, I can appreciate the value of getting good grades in school. If I'd had better grades when I was in school, I might have been accepted to play basketball at a UCLA or a USC. Good grades, at the very least, give you extra choices in life. And that's what I'd preach to Sidney.

My own personal downfall began in 1987. I was just walking off a curb on Pacific Avenue when three black girls made a sharp turn with their car going across 16th and sent me flying about seventy feet down the street. Somehow, I remained conscious the whole time. And although badly injured, I was determined to play sports again. The injury was to my shins. I still have screws in my shins as a result of that accident. I've never fully recovered, but, because of therapy, was able to play in the Gay Men's Softball League again six or seven months later.

I dread to think what I would have done had I not been able to run again. I don't think I could have ever coached. I've always been a doer, a participant. My joy was in running, hitting, jumping. To sit and watch others doing those things would have probably killed me. Many of my friends and I all had a tremendous amount of respect for our bodies and took care of them so we could keep up with our athletics. Other than sports, I really didn't have another life. I had no other serious career aspirations. Being an athlete was my life. It was tough enough realizing that I would now have to live the rest of my life in pain and be limited in my playing abilities. But at that time, I couldn't even envision not playing at all.

From that point on, however, playing sports meant paying a price. And that price was increased pain in my legs. I started doing coke again and it helped me walk. The cocaine took the pain away. I used it like I would regular prescribed drugs. The coke would give me the feeling that I could fly. I don't make excuses for my drug use at that time. But I was having a tremendous amount of both mental and physical agony after the accident. The coke was used medically. It never made me a bad person. And it never brought about distance in my relationship with the Lord.

To this day, I'm not bitter with those three girls. I've just kind of picked myself up the best way I've known how, and dealt with it. I don't hold a grudge with anybody.

Unfortunately for me, California narcotics officers have never shared my philosophy of using cocaine as a pain reliever. Hence, my cocaine use ended up landing me in prison . . . three times. My original crime was being caught with some coke at this house party over at a girlfriend's place. I had some coke rolled up in my sock, and these officers raided her house. I guess the narcs got tipped off by somebody. They took my coke and my money and gave me a citation that said I needed to report to their office. I never reported. I guess I figured at the time that I might be able to get out of facing the music by not reporting. Bad idea! You see, I was already on parole for another minor incident with the law, and because I didn't report for my probation, they caught up with me and threw me in prison. I just had a bad habit of not reporting to the authorities when I was required to.

I realized and accepted the fact I had broken the law. I was terrified, and knew I was going to have to do time.

Prison was hell! I was sent down like my wings were clipped. You can't do shit when you're in prison. And it didn't matter what you were in for. So there I was, convicted of failing to report to probation twice, and being stuck with drug smugglers, murderers, and rapists. It was pretty horrific, to say the least. But that was just a part of my four months in jail. The other part was the fear.

The fear sinks in when you realize you have to choose between hanging with one group over the others or something's going to come down. And if they find out you're gay, they try to use you sexually. I mean, they'd try to take my food and make me perform sexual acts with them. That's sick enough. But just the point of being locked down like that is awful. And I couldn't have picked a worse time to be locked in some place.

I was in prison during the big earthquake San Francisco had in 1989. It shook our fucking building! I don't know how, but it did. The inmates became frightened and started going off. And things got even worse when we realized that some of the exit doors weren't opening. Afterward, we all signed a petition. The petition stated how we were all stuck in our cages like guinea pigs with nowhere to go in case something happened. Shit, those security guards wouldn't have had enough time to get us all out even if there was no malfunction with the doors. Most of the guys would have been dead by the time they attempted to get us out. The walls would have caved in on us.

Thank God they didn't. But that facility didn't care about our petition or our lives. They treated everyone like cattle. It just didn't matter what you were in for. I wasn't a criminal. I never hurt anybody. But I was stuck with people that I didn't belong with anyway.

After jail, things were never quite the same. I would get kicked out of bars because I didn't have any money. And people became nasty toward me. When I got down on my luck, others would pick fights with me. Believe me, 90 percent of them weren't my fault. Most of them were just started by assholes kicking a guy when he's down. At the time, I was basically homeless. But it was homeless by choice. I didn't stay with anyone because I didn't want people to know what I was doing. I needed total freedom in my life, even if it meant living on the streets.

I never panhandled in a traditional sense as the reporters have written about me in recent months. I would just hit people up that I knew for some money. And I knew a lot of people in the Castro. Like I've mentioned, the Castro is like a big neighborhood where everybody knows everybody else. I probably felt worse than I should have for asking people for money. After all, they were a lot of the same people that I had helped out over the years. But to save face, I usually would tell those people that I just needed the money "as a loan." That I would pay them back.

Eventually I got tired of living on the street and went back to Oakland to stay with Lutha. My family hated my living on the streets, and Lutha kept insisting I live with her and her kids. So I took her up on it.

But my luck didn't really change for the better. In January of 1993, I tested positive for AIDS. I hadn't even realized beforehand that I was HIV positive. I had some of the normal symptoms, but just never wanted to get tested. When I found out, the first thing I thought of was "Man, I have an eighty percent chance of dying from this thing."

After learning far more about the disease now that I have it, I know my chances of survival are zero. I'm so sick right now that I'm ready to die. I want the pain to end. I don't want to put my family out anymore. And I want to join the Lord.

I've known for years what AIDS is. I've known over two hundred people with the disease. Many have died from it, but not my good friend and former teammate Cleo. Rumor had it that Cleo had HIV. But Cleo got murdered around the time I was in prison in 1989. He apparently was going to buy some weed from these dudes in North Richmond. These must have been mean motherfuckers, because when Cleo wouldn't pay what they wanted, one of them shot him from behind while he was tangling with a couple of the others. Otherwise, over a hundred of my friends have died of AIDS. Sometimes I begin to think about exactly how many of my friends and family have died of natural causes. I'll tell you what, it hasn't been very many.

AIDS is the "aquired immune deficiency syndrome." It breaks down your immune system, so opportunistic infections can enter your body. Basically, your body loses its immunity in fending off these diseases.

The earliest AIDS cases in the United States were with young homosexuals around 1981 or so. The disease was pretty much spread by gay men having sex with one another. Because of the way gay men have sex, bleeding often occurs and AIDS is spread through blood. So with young gays sharing partners and going to those fucking bathhouses together in cities like San Francisco, Los Angeles, and New York, AIDS spread like wildfire. I hear that between two-thirds and three-fourths of all reported AIDS cases in the United States today are suffered by homosexual men. Back then, it was probably more like 90 percent.

The shit is getting even scarier these days. Not so much with homosexuals. But with drug-using moms, heterosexuals, and even children. I heard one report saying that there were 100,000 new cases of AIDS reported in 1993, compared to 47,000 in 1992, and 45,000 in 1991. There are now 360,000 people in this country living with AIDS. And 1 in 250 people have HIV. According to a book on the disease, *The AIDS Knowledge Base*, by the year 2000, between 30 and 100 million people worldwide will have been infected by HIV.

Before setting up my doctor's appointment the day I found out I was positive for AIDS, I had many of the symptoms that go along with the disease when it's in its initial stages. Headaches, sore muscles, fevers, throat pains, diarrhea, and so on. I had them all. But those symptoms are nothing compared to what comes next. Not one, but many strains of HIV can enter the body. That's part of the reason many scientists believe there can't possibly be a so-called "magic bullet" that will cure everybody.

But some strains are more popular than others.

AIDS cachexia is known as the AIDS wasting syndrome. This affects more than half of AIDS patients. It's also known as "slim disease," because of all the weight you lose when you get it. My ideal weight is probably around 190 pounds. Right now, I'm down to about 135. If you get cachexia, you will almost definitely die of starvation. Starvation usually occurs when a person is down to two-thirds of their ideal body weight. It's very scary. Personally, I can read the writing on the wall.

About half the people that get cachexia come down with a case of tuberculosis. You might think, "Hey, no problem. TB is treatable in its early stages."

But the problem is, if you already have cachexia, your weight loss has probably dropped too much to have any type of positive response to TB treatment.

Cachexia can work fast at cutting down a person's weight. The average patient loses 5 percent of their body weight within four weeks.

Treatment of cachexia varies from person to person. That's why it's so important to get nutritional counseling from doctors who treat the disease.

Another of the heavy-hitting infections you can get from AIDS is called PCP or pneumonia. This is what Spunky died from. Typically, sufferers start out with chills, fevers, coughs, and lots of sweating.

The effects of the pneumonia are pretty minimal in the beginning. But then the cough worsens and fatigue sets in. Within a few weeks, respiratory problems begin, making it difficult for patients to speak without catching their breath.

When the pneumonia finally hits full force, there's really not a whole lot anyone can do to stop it from taking the patient's life.

There is no cure for AIDS. And every night on TV, I have to listen to the newscasters repeat that fact over and over again. But what they ignore is that there have been many positive strides taken in slowing down the virus' effect on patients. I mean, if I had gotten HIV and AIDS years before I did, I would have died in half the time. I'm still alive today, and that's a direct reflection on the efforts made by scientists in their efforts to find a cure. And hopefully for everybody out there still healthy, they'll listen to all the AIDS prevention education and be careful. Because, man, it's pure hell to have AIDS. Not just to the patient, but to the family and friends as well. I thank the Lord every day for Lutha and everybody else that's helping and praying for me.

I believe that one day they'll find a vaccine for AIDS. It may not be able to help all people, but it'll help most. I just hope they inject the vaccine in the children first. And all the children, not just the so-called privileged ones who have parents with insurance. I remember when measles vaccines weren't readily given to many of the poor and black kids. It was a crime. If you're a kid, you've done absolutely nothing to deserve getting AIDS. I mean, at least if you're an adult, you have a fighting chance to learn the dos and don'ts of prevention.

I would also hope that a vaccine for AIDS wouldn't get caught up in a whole lot of red tape in this country. Between all the health care costs and issues, coming up with the money for a vaccine program could be a problem. It's been tough enough with all the money our government spends on cancer research.

It's ironic, but the first people to get the vaccine will probably be low-risk candidates. The drug users, now one of the leading groups getting AIDS, are both socially and financially undesirable. They'll be the last in line when they should probably be the first.

Hopefully, vaccine or no vaccine, people will start getting the message on how to play it safe out there. The gays have, for the most part, led the march in learning safe methods of having sex with one another. And you hardly ever hear about anyone getting the virus through a blood transfusion anymore. And heterosexuals seem to be coming around, as well. It seems like the major problem is going to be with people who get hooked on that shooting-up shit. Hopefully, that group will wise up and get the fucking message.

My sister Lutha, who is the second oldest of my mother's

eight children, understands me better than anyone else in my family. That's probably a big reason why I'm staying with her now.

Lutha and I have late-night talks together. We talk a lot about the days when we were growing up. I used to wonder what my friends were thinking when I never dated in high school. They must have known I was going to be leading a different lifestyle than the straight and narrow. Then I'll often bring up to Lutha what those friends I had in high school must have thought about me after my homosexuality was publicly revealed in *Inside Sports*.

Lutha just responds with something like "Glenn, you've always been a good person. Whenever me or one of the family was out in public and saw somebody that knew you, they would always ask how you were doing and that you should give them a call."

It really helps to hear Lutha say something like that. Sometimes we'll talk until two or three in the morning. And that's special, because Lutha has to get up at around five. She works as a cook at a local hotel in the mornings and afternoons.

But she never complains. We'll just sit up many nights eating peanut butter or oatmeal and just talk. She never shows me anything but love. I can call for her at any time of the night, and she'll wake up and change my diaper for me. She's great!

And to top it off, she's a single parent raising some terrific kids. I'm the proud uncle to some well-mannered, polite children. And that's a credit to Lutha. She's got the Lord in her heart.

The hardest thing about having AIDS for me, besides the pain, is not being able to get off the bed. I'm trying to learn to sit up and get into the wheelchair on my own, but it's extremely difficult to even try. My feet are causing the problem. You see, the dead skin from my lesions is coming off of them now, and it makes them very sensitive to any pressure I apply to them.

But the problems with my feet are just a small part of the physical and mental anguish that I'm going through as an AIDS patient.

Thank God I have Lutha. That woman's been a saint.

THE SILVER LINING

When I think back to my fucked-up experience with the A's from '78 to '80, it's incredible to see how they've come to my aid in my time of need. Of course, the backbone of that organization has changed tremendously. Finley is long gone, having sold the team some fifteen years ago. And Billy the Kid died five years ago in a car accident in upstate New York. Sandy Alderson and Tony LaRussa now run the franchise. Perhaps not so surprisingly, the A's have become arguably the majors' class organization over the last seven or eight seasons, in part because of the two of them, boasting three trips to the World Series.

Besides their ability to win ball games, the A's have shown a great deal of class in how they've helped their current and former players. When the A's found out my situation, they quickly put together a plan to see that my needs would be taken care of.

My old buddy Jack McGowan actually got the ball rolling. He called the A's president and general manager Sandy Alderson in the spring of '94. Jack was lucky. He got Sandy's secretary, and told the "screener" that one of the A's former ballplayers was very sick. Sandy happened to be free and took the call at his desk. I would imagine that someone of Sandy's importance probably gets dozens of calls from people looking for help or donations, but he took, from what I understand, twenty or so minutes from his busy schedule to speak with Jack about me.

Sandy should have gotten some earplugs, because my boy Jack can talk! Jack told him how I wasn't just anybody, but someone he had known for years and that I had once been a member of the A's.

According to Jack, Sandy said, "Well, I'll tell you what I'm going to do. I'm going to speak with one of my front office people, Pamela Pitts, and have her contact you and see what we can do to help Glenn."

So Sandy apparently walked right down to her office and said, "Pamela, I have something for you to do."

Pamela, the team's director of baseball administration, was told of my plight and called Jack back almost immediately to set up a strategy.

Setting up strategies to help people in need wasn't anything new to Pamela. That girl's got a heart of gold! She once helped out a former A's pitcher named Mark Stancel who was stricken with brain cancer the winter after his last season in Oakland in

1991. Pamela organized several fund-raisers on Stancel's behalf in places like Modesto, as well as at the sites of all the A's minor-league teams.

Sandy should be given a lot of credit too. I mean, even though I've never met the man, he is, after all, the guy that gives the okay to Pamela to do these things. Pamela told me that even though Sandy will tell her the A's can't save the world and help everybody in need, they'll always do what they can.

Sandy and Pamela really seem to take life's important things to heart. If I had only played for the A's today instead of fifteen years ago, things would have been much different. Even their current manager, Tony LaRussa, seems to be a fair guy. And he's proven you can be both fair and successful. He's perhaps the brightest manager in the game today.

Part of Pamela's strategy was to start making phone calls. She spoke with both the Association of Pro Ballplayers and the Baseball Assistance Team (BAT). Both organizations were interested in helping out financially. Pamela was immediately sent $500 from the Association of Pro Ballplayers for my food and bus-pass expenses. I was still splitting my time crashing with friends in the Castro and over in Oakland with Lutha. By August of '94, it had become increasingly difficult to get my ass off the couch. The AIDS was becoming a crippling thing. So Pamela spent some of the money she received on my behalf to buy me a cordless phone.

The Association of Ballplayers sent Pamela another $500 the following month. By around this time, I was living with

Lutha full-time. So Pamela would send Lutha the money for me whenever I needed it.

The bills started piling up, and Pamela went to Joe Garagiola, who runs the Baseball Assistance Team.

Garagiola was eager to help out, and that's kind of an ironic thing. Garagiola has had a longtime affiliation and friendship with Lasorda, who, to say the least, probably looks at me as kind of a thorn in his life. But Garagiola's a class guy. He's always looked at the game of major-league baseball like it should be looked at: a kid's game played by men. He's always quoted as saying, "You've got to have a lot of little boy in you to play this game!"

And he's right. It apparently doesn't bother Garagiola that Glenn Burke is gay. He probably sees me as an ex–major leaguer that's gotten a few tough breaks in his life. Period. And he just wants to help.

Garagiola's company donated $500 to help my cause.

As you can probably imagine, the generosity of these organizations hasn't been enough to pay for all of my medical and living expenses. Fortunately, the government has been a big help as well. Because I'm considered "indigent," the government takes care of the majority of my medical bills. I'm lucky in this respect. A lot of AIDS patients have great difficulties getting the needed funds to pay their bills. So I guess despite all the shit that's happened to me, there has been a silver lining.

Another part of that silver lining has been the Welcome Home Restaurant in the Castro, a home-cooking kind of place that's open from early in the morning until late at night. In June of '94, Jack and Pamela met with the owner of the Welcome Home, Ray Powers, to work out some kind of arrangement where I could eat there whenever I wanted free of charge. The money that Pamela was receiving from the organizations would pay for it. The A's wouldn't just give me the money. I guess they figured I might spend it on drugs. So Pamela and Ray worked out their own little system. Ray would notify his staff that whenever I came in the restaurant that I could order anything I wanted off the menu and I'd sign my name on the bill. When my alloted dollars ran up, they'd call Pam and ask her to send them a check. They might call Pamela every week to two weeks and tell her that she owed $100 or $75 and that they've added 15 percent for the waiting staff. Pamela would then get off a check. They didn't know Pamela from "the man on the moon," but they knew Jack. And they knew me. So everything went pretty smoothly.

Although I was spending a lot of my time then with a friend of mine named Alex, I remained elusive. I was crashing all over the Castro. But like I mentioned before, the Castro is the biggest little section of any city I know. So tracking me down wasn't too hard. In fact, the first time I ever met Pamela, I had to be tracked down by Jack's network of friends. Jack just kind of walked the streets trying to locate me and told just about everyone he saw that if they saw me to let me know that both he and Pam from the Oakland A's wanted to meet me at the Welcome Home Restaurant later that afternoon. Like I said, I would just bum around the Castro. But one of the people he spoke to let me know of their whereabouts. That Castro is just such a neat community.

Jack and Pamela had been sitting in there for a half hour or so when I kind of shuffled into the restaurant. Sure enough, there was Jack with this woman who had a big smile on her face. Pamela said enthusiastically, "You must be Glenn!"

She stood right up and gave me a big hug and I remember feeling all kinds of things emotionally. At first, I gave her one of my big, broken-tooth grins. Then, I just burst out into tears. They were tears of joy.

I could tell that Pamela may have been taken aback with my appearance. After all, she knew me as a onetime professional big leaguer who went by the nickname of King Kong. And here I was, pretty emaciated at that point from the AIDS.

She explained in further detail what the A's wanted to do for me, and I was extremely touched. I just said again and again, "I can't believe you want to help me."

Pamela responded with "My God, Glenn, if I were in your predicament, I would hope to God someone would have the heart to help me too."

But I knew better. First, I was overjoyed with all of Jack's efforts in making the A's aware of my situation. And then I was equally impressed with how gracious the A's were being with their support. Just thinking about the heart that those two people have shown me makes me want to cry all over again.

Jack and Pamela have become kind of like a team for me as

well. A lot of times, when Pamela comes over here to Lutha's house to visit, she picks up Jack at the BART station. Pamela clearly does far more than what's required of her from the A's. We have become great friends. She often brings me little gifts. And the two of them are so patient with me. A lot of times when they visit me, I'll just drift off to sleep. But they don't mind. They'll just go sit in the living room until I wake up again. I try my hardest to stay awake, but between the medication and the virus itself, it's a real challenge. I also try to be in good spirits even when I'm in horrible agony. But that's also hard, and I feel badly if I sometimes seem a little rude. I'll tell people, "I'm sorry, but I'm just in a bad mood right now."

And everyone's so beautiful. They all seem to understand.

Another thing about those two. When they're not here, they call me all the time to check up on me. I'm not always able to talk on the phone, but it's nice to know people are thinking about me. It's one of the reasons I fight on with this disease.

In fact, since I've been sick, it's hard to believe how many of my old friends and other well-wishers have contacted me. Some people aren't open-minded when it comes to homosexuality. But sometimes we underestimate people. I used to think my schoolmates thought I wasn't all right or I wasn't cool if I turned out to be gay. But that hasn't been true even in a single case. *All* of my friends came back to check on me at one time or another over the past few months. And 50 to 60 percent of them said, "We knew you were gay, but you were our friend anyway. And we loved you."

Or "We wish you hadn't disappeared," alluding to my years of living in the Castro.

It had been twenty or thirty years since I had seen many of my Oakland friends. These were the friendships that came from the heart first and foremost. They apparently never cared that I turned out gay. We had love first, and I've learned that nothing, particularly becoming gay, can ever take that away from people.

It's funny about old friends. When you need them most, they're always there for you. It's actually sad that we often have to go through something painful to find out who our true friends really are. It shouldn't have to be that way.

The other well-wishers have come to know my story through a recent media explosion about my life. I must admit, the response from both the media and supporters has really been a pleasant surprise. I didn't expect it and it has really helped. My current plight has been written about in every major paper across the country, including features in the *New York Times*, the *San Francisco Chronicle*, and the *Los Angeles Times*. It's been in magazines, including nice write-ups in *People* and *Baseball Weekly*. And some twenty writers and two movie companies have approached me about obtaining the copyright to my life story. I chose a freelance writer from New York to write this book with me because his proposal of my life was very detailed. He did a thorough job of what we needed to talk about and that's important to someone in my condition. Time is of the essence. I couldn't guarantee any writer more than a day at a time.

None of the articles have really captured me for the man I am. They've tended to dwell on the negatives of my life, like the drugs and prison time. And most of the articles have included things totally untrue about me. One article had Jack finding me practically incoherent in some gutter. I mean, that shit's just ridiculous. I guess certain writers feel like they have to spice up their articles with good lies to sell newspapers. That was one of the reasons I wanted to write this book. I wanted to set the record straight about my life. I might not have always been an angel, but I never did anything to intentionally hurt anyone.

I hope people have the courage to pick up and read this book. Not because of the money. After all, there's a chance I won't be around when this book goes public and won't see any of the money anyway. What's most important to me is my wish that people will learn about the hypocrisy that exists in baseball and it's "fear" of homosexuality that had me blackballed from professional baseball. It's fucking ignorant.

I realize this isn't the first book of its kind. Dave Pallone, the former umpire, was blackballed as well for being homosexual, and wrote about it in *Behind the Mask*. But I'm the first and only gay ballplayer to have been blackballed from baseball. And whereas Pallone had a full career umpiring, I was never given the chance once in the majors to show what I was fully capable of producing on the ball field. Many people I've talked with agree: it's a bigger story than if some superstar like Reggie Jackson came out and said he was gay. It's a bigger story because at least somebody like Reggie had his career. That's the biggest injustice. And that's the story. The hypocrisy of baseball. You conform to their system by, say, getting married, and you can still play. But if you don't conform to their system, you can't play and that's fucked up. I mean, if I can hit the curveball, what the hell's the difference who I'm sleeping with?

I haven't been in the major leagues for fifteen years, so I can't be a hundred percent sure that the game's attitude toward gays hasn't improved. I mean, I can see signs of things getting better. Just look at what the A's are doing for me.

The Dodgers, though, remain a question mark in this regard. My old friend Vincent Trahan saw Lasorda while visiting his son at his ninth-grade graduation ceremony about two years ago. The Dodgers and Trahan were staying at the same Marriott Hotel in San Diego. I know my man Vincent wanted to tell Tommy off for the shit he put me through years ago, but he was cool enough to know it wasn't his place to do that. So, instead, Vincent walked up to Tommy and said, "Mr. Lasorda, I'm a good friend of Glenn Burke's, and I don't know if you know Glenn's situation right now, but I told him if I ever saw you again, I would tell you that Glenn said hello."

Lasorda's face apparently changed several colors, and after a pause to think of something appropriate to say, he said, "Tell Glenn that I asked about him and that he should hang in there."

Clearly, I believe, Lasorda was shocked that one of my boys would be so cordial with him and that I didn't harbor any bitter feelings toward him anymore. Lasorda probably expected Vincent to say something like "Hey, motherfucker, you screwed with my boy Glenn's career. Kiss my ass!"

But that would have been the wrong thing to say.

Lasorda's body language, according to Vincent, showed some concern for me, but there was also a distance. Tommy's got to still have some remorse for not doing the right thing by me. After all, Tommy's a Christian. He may not share his remorse with people over what he did to me, but I'm sure when the time comes when he sees or hears of my passing, his remorse may become magnified toward himself.

Lasorda is still apparently in denial over the cause of Spunky's death. If you hear him talk about it, Spunky died of regular pneumonia, not AIDS-related pneumonia. He never talks outwardly about his son being involved in the gay world.

Spunky's death is tough on Lasorda. Think what you will about Tommy, but it's very tough on any man to bury his son. It's an awful thing. So if "denial" is how Lasorda chooses to deal with his son's death, that's his choice. But it's kind of a flip with his Catholic religion and all the "We don't judge, God judges" testament that the Church teaches its congregation. After all, we're supposed to love on this earth. But in sports, that machismo still exists.

In the real world, it's different. You can say, "Well, it's okay that this guy's gay because he's a fucking shoe salesman. But not Hercules, the middle linebacker for the Championship 49er's. No way! There may be, at best, slightly less homophobia in sports than there used to be, but don't think for a minute that there aren't scores of athletes that remain in the closet. That shit will never end.

The over three hundred letters that I've received have all been ones of encouragement. They tell me about the positive impact I've had on the writers' lives. They make me feel like I was sent to this earth to make certain people happier. It's amazing. That's what breaks me up now, makes me cry and stuff like that. It's an example of some of the love I gave to people through my life and through my story.

Sometimes the letters come here at Lutha's house and sometimes they go to Pamela's office. The letters just keep right on coming. And I read each and every one of them. They really help me. When I finish reading them, I feel weak. Nobody is forcing these people to write to me. They don't have to do this. You can tell their words come from their heart. That's the only way they can write the stuff like they do. They couldn't write like they have if they didn't truly care about me.

One of the great things about being a Christian is having a heart that's over-happy. It's like you want to give energy back to other people. You want to let others know that if everybody tried, this world would be beautiful. The trees would be growing, the grass would be cut, the flowers would be blooming. It would be like the first day of spring every day. Nobody would have to worry about being robbed. Blacks and whites would get along better. Shit, it really bothers me that blacks and whites can't get along better. It just doesn't have to be the way it is today. We could have heaven on earth if everybody tried. But for some reason, we can't have that. Too many knuckleheads, I guess.

Besides the support of friends and well-wishers, the holding out of some hope for a cure of AIDS also keeps me going. I mean, you've got to pray for a miracle when you're in my condition. And I have received some good news of late. My doctor said that he might give radiation treatment to my feet which, as I mentioned, are practically covered with black lesions.

Positive thinking and the love of others has been my most reliable medicine. Medical people who deal with AIDS patients every day didn't give me past Christmas of '94. So as unsettling as it may sound, I'm on borrowed time! Every morning that I wake up, it's a gift from the Lord. If everyone saw their life like that, it would be a far better world. Believe me.

On November 15, 1994, my loving friends gave me a tribute dinner at Geoffrey's Inner Circle in Oakland. Many Berkeley athletes from my youth were there, like Trahan, Rusty Jackson, Johnny Burks, "Shooty" Babitt, and Gene Ransom. Even my old buddy Marvin Webb was there. Marvin is now into so many different things. After being released from the Seattle Mariners organization, he became very involved with the Bay Area community. He's now a minister at Peniel Church in San Pablo and works as an associate scout with the A's. He gets paid only if he introduces the A's to a player they eventually sign to a contract. And he gets to see a lot of different young players. He's the hitting instructor at Contra Costa Junior College. But he tells me all the time how the young players of today are different from when we played in the seventies. He says they don't want to play hard or get their uniforms dirty like we did. But he lives his life knowing what's most important, and that's living the life that the Lord wants us to live. To not judge, but to accept others as they are. After all, we are all sinners.

The former A's outfielder Mike Davis also showed up, and Dusty Baker would have made it except for some type of meeting having to do with the current baseball strike.

"The Glenn Burke Tribute," as they called it, was a beautiful occasion. There was great food and drinks, a live band, and film footage of my life. Unfortunately, I was only able to appear for maybe five minutes. My sisters wheeled me out into the room in my wheelchair. I sobbed and sobbed, even as I gave my speech thanking everyone for coming. I was just so cold and in so much pain. I was just having a particularly bad week with the AIDS.

In fact, two nights later, my Berkeley High School jersey was to be retired on the opening night of the school's basketball season. They were going to have a big ceremony in my honor. But I couldn't make that occasion at all. It's awful to have to die like I am right now. Here I have all of these people going out of their way to show me how much they care and I can't even make an appearance anymore.

Despite my efforts to fight off this horrible disease, I know that I'll soon be in heaven with the Lord. And I'll be rejoining so many of my friends who have died before me. I'll be seeing my two best friends again, Manny Simmons and Wes Jackson. I'll be seeing my sister again. And the Lord will take away all the pain I'm in right now.

As I reach my final days, I'd like to be remembered as just a down-to-earth good person. A man that tried to never have a bad thought in his mind. A man who really tried to get along with everybody at all times, no matter what the situation. A man who will always love his great friends and family.

Despite what people are going to say or write about me after I die, I want it to be known that I have no regrets about how I lived my life. I did the best I could.

Well, maybe I do have just one regret. I should have been a basketball player!

AFTERWORD

The phone call I received on the afternoon of May 30, 1995, was expected, one that was simply a matter of when it would be made, not if. That was just the way things went in the earlier days of the AIDS epidemic.

"Erik," a soft, quivering voice from the usually high-energized, diamond-in-the-rough Oakland A's administrator Pamela Pitts started. "I have some sad news. Glenn passed away a little while ago."

My initial reaction was that all too common combination of deep sadness and relief for a friend or loved one that suffers intense pain near the end of their life. The sadness comes in knowing that a life like Glenn's that began with endless possibilities had been cut short at just forty-two years. Conversely, the relief came in knowing that Glenn would now be in peace and would no longer have the unbearable pain he had been enduring.

The service at Fouche's Hudson Funeral Home in Oakland took place on a typically sunny Northern California morning before a packed, standing room–only congregation of Glenn's friends and family. I sat with Pamela, the woman whom then Oakland A's general manager Sandy Alderson had tasked with making sure Glenn would receive meals at the Welcome Home Restaurant in the Castro section of San Francisco while homeless. It was during those meals that Pamela and Glenn developed a close bond and a relationship that she still treasures to this day. Pamela was the only representative from Major League Baseball to attend the service, sadly a sign of the times.

I glanced over to the other side of the room and caught a glimpse of Glenn's mother, who sat facing forward in frozen silence, a woman who was now enduring the second funeral of a child. I thought how no parent should have to suffer the loss of even one child let alone two. It was one of the saddest sights I have ever seen.

But nothing could prepare me or anyone else in the congregation emotionally for what would come later in the service. First came a recording from the music group the Hollies, playing their song "He Ain't Heavy, He's My Brother." Then Glenn's siblings sang along in front of where he lay. The song, which is about carrying a brother's burden, left not a dry eye in the room. I can still hear that song playing in my head. I still get emotional about it.

How appropriate the choice was for Glenn's sister Lutha to take part in the singing of that particular song. If there are angels on this earth, she is one of them. When Glenn was sick and homeless, she went out looking for him, brought him home, and was his caregiver during the final year of his life. When Glenn needed frequent breaks from my interviews with him at Lutha's house, she couldn't have been a more gracious host. She was clearly glad that Glenn was under her care, and her disposition was always upbeat.

Lutha and I stayed in touch for a while following the funeral as much as being on separate coasts of the United States would allow, and I never lost the sense of her love for her brother. At her request, I sent her audiotapes of some of the interviews I did with Glenn because she deeply missed the sound of his voice. The tapes are a difficult listen, as Glenn can be heard at times crying from the pain he was in. Still, it was my hope that hearing Glenn's voice would give Lutha some comfort and perhaps even fill part of the void that her brother's passing brought to her.

These days, Lutha lives with whichever of her four grown children need her the most. Her spirit of giving and caring continues on today.

The book you hold in your hands, one that I originally self-published in 1995, represented a promise I made to Glenn that the story of his life would be on the record. While Glenn did read a final draft of the manuscript, his passing sadly came just weeks before the release of the book. Seeing one's life story in a book can be a surreal experience, but the importance of

Glenn's words would take on special meaning. This is more than an autobiography, but also a time capsule of the social attitudes toward gays in the baseball world and society both during and following Glenn's days in the major leagues.

Glenn was the first professional athlete in the four major North American sports to be openly gay. When the two clubs he played for, the Los Angeles Dodgers and the Oakland A's, found out about his lifestyle, they quickly sought to move him off their respective teams. In the Dodgers' case, it was a trade to Oakland for an aging Billy North. In Oakland, it was twofold. First, it was manager Billy Martin's homophobic remarks toward Glenn in front of his teammates and coaches that created, to say the least, a hostile work environment. Then a demotion to the minor leagues effectively buried Glenn's prospects for a future in baseball.

As Glenn's "mouthpiece" through the numerous interviews and lectures I've given over the last two decades, the question I have been most frequently asked has been what managers would have been able or willing to coach a gay ballplayer on their club. While it is hard to see inside the mind of individual managers, the one I always thought, without question, would have been open-minded enough to do it would have been Glenn's former Dodger teammate Dusty Baker.

In the nearly twenty years since Glenn's death, I have had the pleasure on several occasions of sitting in Dusty's manager's office or watching batting practice with him when he piloted first the San Francisco Giants and later the Cincinnati Reds, to talk about the young man he referred to as "my son." He liked Glenn before he found out he was gay, and those feelings didn't change a bit after he knew.

We seldom talked about the "high five" Glenn famously gave to Dusty in 1977 after his thirtieth home run of that season, widely credited as the very first one ever given. Instead, we talked about what Glenn meant to the Dodgers and their clubhouse chemistry. And we discussed how much the two men enjoyed each other's time away from the field. It was the classic case of the veteran role model showing the way to a young and up-and-coming teammate.

As for the players themselves, many of Glenn's Dodger teammates seemed to be fine with playing with a gay player. As Davey Lopes told the media the day after Glenn was traded, "He was the life of the team—on the buses, in the clubhouse, everywhere."

It was clear that the players just wanted to win no matter what a teammate did on his own time. On the hyper-talented Dodger teams of the late seventies, what a player did on the field, for the most part, superseded everything else. Those were the days when the money earned from winning a World Series would be a significant percentage of a ballplayer's take-home pay. Taking as an example the year of 1977, when the Dodgers went to the World Series with Glenn as a member of the team, the average major-league salary was $74,000. The World Series winner that season took home over $27,000, the loser nearly $21,000. Thus, it was much more than just the glory of winning the Fall Classic that mattered back then.

Today, with multimillion-dollar contracts in play, the economics of winning a championship have changed drastically. In 2013, the average salary in baseball was $3.4 million. When the Red Sox won the World Series, they each took home an additional $307,000, far less than what the average player made in base salary. This is not to insinuate that players don't work just as hard to win the World Series, but at least economically the fact remains that there is less financial incentive.

So with the economies being less of a factor, what challenges would a gay baseball player face today?

There is still the perceived morality issue that some of the more religious players might have with playing with a homosexual. For others, there could be a feeling of being uncomfortable sharing a locker room with an openly gay teammate. And then there would be the fans, many of which can be brutal to players under normal circumstances, much less extenuating situations like if a gay ballplayer were on the field.

Still, I can't help but get the sense that things would be different and far better if a baseball player came out today than back in Glenn's playing days. Social attitudes have changed dramatically in just the last few years, which Glenn likely would not have thought possible in his lifetime.

The first major shift in sentiment came with the 2011 overturning of the US military's Don't Ask, Don't Tell policy that was put into effect during the Clinton administration in 1993. The policy prohibited military personnel from discriminating against or harassing closeted homosexual or bisexual service members or applicants, while barring openly gay, lesbian, or bisexual persons from military service. Thus, gays could serve in the military as long as they kept their orientation a secret.

Since Don't Ask, Don't Tell ended, persons who are openly homosexual and bisexual have been able to serve.

So what drove this change in military policy? Clearly, it was an overwhelming shift in public opinion. A year prior to the overhaul of Don't Ask, Don't Tell, a *Washington Post*/ABC News poll revealed that 77 percent of Americans said gays and lesbians who publicly disclosed their orientation should be allowed to serve in the armed forces. The support was surprisingly widespread across all political parties in the survey, with Democrats showing 86 percent approval of homosexuals serving openly and Republicans coming in at 74 percent. Perhaps most eye-opening was how 70 percent of white evangelical Protestants were in favor of gays serving in the military.

Other surveys backed up the findings of the *Washington Post*/ABC News poll. During the same time period in 2010, the Pew Research Center found that 58 percent of people in the United States approved of gays serving openly in the military, with only 27 percent opposed. And a CNN/Opinion Research Corporation poll showed 72 percent of Americans in support of the overhaul of Don't Ask, Don't Tell, with just 23 percent opposing it.

It was becoming clear that equal treatment for our servicemen and servicewomen now trumped what people had considered a moral issue.

Next came the overturning of California's Prop 8, the high-profile same-sex marriage provision. The proposition was originally created by opponents of same-sex marriage, with their belief that only marriage between a man and a woman should be valid.

In *Perry v. Schwarzenegger*, Prop 8 was ultimately ruled unconstitutional by a federal court in 2010, with United States District Court Judge Vaughn Walker ruling that it violated both the due process and the equal protection clauses of the US Constitution. After an unsuccessful appeal, the court's decision went into effect in 2013.

Again, this represents a seismic shift in sentiment toward gays not just in California, but throughout the country. Before 2004, same-sex marriage was not performed in any US state. By 2014, nineteen states were issuing marriage licenses to gay couples, with three states creating legal unions for same-sex partners. The number of states is sure to grow, as the United States Court of Appeals is actively involved in hearing same-sex marriage cases.

It was also during this period that President Obama became the first United States president to declare his support of same-sex marriage, a reversal from his stance in 2008 when he cited his beliefs as a Christian that marriage was a "sacred union" between a man and a woman.

Gay rights and tolerance then began spilling over into the sports world. In May of 2013, twelve-year NBA center Jason

Collins came out in a *Sports Illustrated* cover story where he exclaimed, "I didn't set out to be the first openly gay athlete in a major American team sport. But since I am, I'm happy to start the conversation."

While no one would mistake Collins for a superstar, he was still a big man who played tough defense, a valuable commodity for any club. In some respects, appropriately enough, he was like Glenn in that he was a superb athlete who was used more as a role player. And also like Glenn, he played on winning teams, being a part of two state high school championships, the NCAA Final Four, and the Elite Eight, as well as participating in nine play-offs in his twelve NBA seasons.

At the time of the *Sports Illustrated* exclusive, Collins was a free agent looking for a team. Thus, I actually believe the eventual news of his signing with the Brooklyn Nets nearly nine months later was just as big, if not a bigger, story than his coming out, because a club was now activating the first publicly known gay player ever in the four major North American sports.

Furthermore, I felt the fact that the Nets' press release didn't even make mention about Collins being gay spoke volumes. His sexual orientation was being treated as a private matter as far as the Nets were concerned and rightfully so.

The announcement went as follows:

The Brooklyn Nets have signed center Jason Collins to a 10-day contract, General Manager Billy King announced today.

"The decision to sign Jason was a basketball decision," said King.
"We needed to increase our depth inside, and with his experience
and size, we felt he was the right choice for a 10-day contract."
Collins will be available for tonight's game versus the Los
Angeles Lakers.

So what led Collins to come out after all those years? In the
Sports Illustrated article, Collins wrote, "I realized I needed to
go public when Joe Kennedy, my old roommate at Stanford and
now a Massachusetts congressman, told me he had just
marched in Boston's Gay Pride Parade. I'm seldom jealous of
others, but hearing what Joe had done filled me with envy. I
was proud of him for participating but angry that as a closeted
gay man I couldn't even cheer my straight friend on as a spec-
tator. If I'd been questioned, I would have concocted half-
truths. What a shame to have to lie at a celebration of pride. I
want to do the right thing and not hide anymore. I want to
march for tolerance, acceptance and understanding. I want to
take a stand and say, 'Me, too.'"

Billy Jean King, one of the greatest tennis stars of all time
and one of the first openly gay athletes, put the gay movement
in perfect context when she was quoted in the same edition of
Sports Illustrated as saying, "You've got to push, one by one by
one, all the time, to get a little movement. And then eventually
there's that tipping point, where it's more of a cascade. From
glacier to flood."

Around the time that the Nets signed Collins, the next athlete to come out was Michael Sam, a football all-American defensive lineman from Missouri and the Associated Press SEC Defensive Player of the Year. By coming out just months before the NFL draft, Sam was truly risking his future NFL career before it even began, not to mention millions of dollars in contract money. That was because many in the sport wondered if his announcement would affect the round in which he would get drafted, or whether he would get drafted at all.

So why did he take the risk that he did at that critical juncture of his career?

"I didn't realize how many people actually knew, and I was afraid that someone would tell or leak something about me," he told ESPN. "I want to own my truth. No one else should tell my story but me."

Although he had already come out to his Missouri teammates the prior year, making the public announcement about his sexual orientation was a major step.

But in the "tipping point" that Billy Jean King had alluded to, Sam has received support where he needed it most.

First, it was his Missouri coach, Gary Pinkel, who said in a statement, "We're really happy for Michael that he's made the decision to announce this, and we're proud of him and how he represents Mizzou. He's a great example of just how important it is to respect others. He's taught a lot of people here firsthand that it doesn't matter what your background is, or your personal orientation, we're all on the same team and we all support each other."

The NFL mirrored those sentiments with a statement from its senior vice president of communications, Greg Aiello, when he said, "Michael is a football player. Any player with ability and determination can succeed in the NFL. We look forward to welcoming and supporting Michael Sam in 2014."

But perhaps Sam said it best himself: "I'm not afraid to tell the world who I am. I'm Michael Sam. I'm a college graduate. I'm African American. And I'm gay. I'm comfortable in my skin."

And now, after being drafted in the seventh round of the 2014 draft by the St. Louis Rams and later joining the Dallas Cowboys as a member of their practice squad, he is an openly gay player in the NFL. Is the tide turning in football? A recent ESPN.com survey would certainly make it seem so. A poll of the top three hundred high school football recruits in the nation revealed that nearly 73 percent of the respondents said they would have no issue selecting a college program with an openly gay player on the roster. The recruits represent the near future of the NFL and signal an environment of inclusion among the ranks. This will only make it easier for future Michael Sams to come out.

What has been amazing to me is the speed at which all of the latest milestones have taken place. From Glenn's passing in 1995 up until the 2011 overturning of Don't Ask, Don't Tell, there was truly little progress in the gay movement. But over the last several years, it seems like there has been some new development nearly every time you pick up the newspaper.

Perhaps in a prelude of what was to come, in the summer of 2010, my old friend Pamela Pitts called to tell me a documentary was being made by Comcast about Glenn's life. Sean Maddison, one of the producers of the film, *Out: The Glenn Burke Story*, wanted to meet with me in New York for an on-camera interview. Speaking by phone, I told him I would be honored to be a part of any project to do with Glenn.

I was impressed immediately by Maddison's enthusiasm for the project and his attention to detail. He had become an expert on Glenn's life and, along with colleague and documentarian Doug Harris, had filmed interviews with an impressive lineup of men who had either watched Glenn play or were teammates of his. Some of those teammates, according to Glenn in my interviews with him, weren't always so friendly with him during their playing days. But as is evident in the film, they had clearly come around and gained a better understanding of some of the challenges Glenn faced during his baseball career.

The documentary was released in November of 2010 in a red-carpet premiere at the Castro Theatre in San Francisco. As photographers' bulbs flashed outside, a woman came out of nowhere and gave me a long and tight embrace. It was Lutha. It had been many years since we had seen one another, and it meant the world to me to see her again.

....

Once inside the theater, I came to realize this would be a star-studded affair. One of the greatest linebackers of all-time, Bill Romanowski, was on one side of the VIP room. The Oakland Raiders' quarterback at the time, Jason Campbell, was on the other. They were there with other professional athletes to do an onstage debate and discussion following the viewing of the documentary, on whether or not openly gay athletes would one day be accepted in their respective sports. A high-profile conversation had begun.

Watching the documentary was a surreal experience for me. One after another, former Dodger teammates like Dusty Baker, Reggie Smith, Rick Monday, and Dave Lopes, and A's teammates like Rickey Henderson and Claudell Washington, as well as scouts, coaches, and friends of Glenn's, backed up all the incredibly hard-to-comprehend travails Glenn shared with me during interviews with him. Glenn's recall of events from his playing days—the good, the bad, and the ugly—turned out to be 100 percent accurate. My decision to move forward with a self-published book—risks and all—was reaffirmed by what I was watching on the big screen. There was a sense of relief after fifteen years that getting his story out there had turned out to be an important part of sports history.

I became a part of the documentary during some of the more emotional moments of the film when Glenn's voice could be heard from the tapes of the interviews I did with him. I wasn't previously aware that Comcast would use the tapes in the documentary, and hearing Glenn's voice again—at times through his sobbing because of the unbearable pain he was experiencing—jolted me like a lightning bolt. It was heartbreaking to watch, and choking up inside, I had to do everything I could to keep it together. You could have heard a pin drop in the theater during the times when Glenn's voice was heard. I feel the use of those sound bites from Glenn took the documentary to another level.

Harris told the *Contra Costa Times*, "It would be nice if viewers look at this film and take a personal assessment of their whole level of acceptance, not necessarily dealing just with the gay issue but acceptance overall."

The publicity generated from the documentary and a series of feature stories about what Glenn's story said about our society drove some interest from Hollywood. For actress Jamie Lee Curtis, it was an article in *The Week* about Glenn's life and the advent of the high five that initially stirred her interest in the making of a movie based on this book. Jamie Lee has worked diligently for several years in trying to get a film made. With the successful momentum of the gay movement in recent years, and with Glenn more and more being recognized as the first openly gay athlete in the four major North American sports, it would seem to be just a matter of time before her goal becomes a reality.

I gave a lecture at the Yogi Berra Museum about Glenn in the winter of 2014. The museum, fittingly enough, has an exhibit dedicated to inclusion in sports that features phrases like "Treat everyone the same" and "Respect the game, Respect others." The talk sparked the attention of Athlete Ally, a non-profit organization that educates and activates athletic communities to eliminate homophobia and transphobia in sports.

Athlete Ally and the Yogi Berra Museum had formed a partnership in 2013. Through an introduction by museum director David Kaplan, I met with Samantha Marchiano, who is on the board of directors for Athlete Ally, to discuss ways we could use Glenn's story to create awareness about the importance of both equality and respect in sports. Several months later, Samantha called with some truly incredible news.

"Major League Baseball would like to honor Glenn at this year's all-star game," Samatha said. "They are interested in flying his sister Lutha to Minnesota for a ceremony. Commissioner Bud Selig will be involved in the presentation. Would you reach out to Lutha and see if this would be of interest to her?"

I could hardly believe what I was hearing. I knew Lutha would be as floored as I was. I told Samantha that I would contact Alice Rose, one of Lutha's daughters, and was confident it could be worked out. Sure enough, Alice accompanied her mother to the all-star game.

At a press conference at the All Star Game Fan Festival, Commissioner Selig recognized Glenn for his early role in the gay sports movement, and also made the announcement that former major leaguer Billy Bean, the only other ballplayer to reveal his homosexuality, would become the first Major League Baseball ambassador of inclusion.

"All-star week is a celebration of our sport," Selig began. "Because of the presence of Lutha and Billy, today is a day for us to celebrate in a very meaningful way. Lutha, I am so delighted that you are here. Your brother was a pioneer. We remember him to this day and we want to tell his story."

Selig continued, "We want the people who make a living in our game to be who they wish to be. As an institution, we will do all we can to support them."

Both Lutha and Bean were given time to give remarks, as well.

"I have no doubt that Glenn would be very happy today," Lutha said. "Because when you are just busy trying to live a life and be a decent human being, and play [baseball] as best you can, with all the respect you can, it should be a done deal or an easy deal. And for that, I would like to thank you very much and thank MLB for having myself and my daughter, to honor or stand in for him. Thank you."

Bean, who will visit and give talks to each of the thirty major-league clubs as part of his new role, said, "I'm very proud that MLB is recognizing the social responsibility and the importance of this decision to provide and ensure an equitable and inclusive workplace. And I want to make sure that everybody understands that the history, the integrity, of baseball is never going to change.

"Today is about getting our young players a chance to understand their responsibility as the role models this league gives them," Bean continued. "They are thrust into a big, shiny, wonderful world as young men, and a lot of them have not been exposed to the same things that all of us outside the game have been. And that's the responsibility that I am going to take very seriously. It's not here to change the way people think, ask you to be friends with someone that you're not friends with; it's just to give everyone who is a part of the MLB family a chance to be the very best they can be."

And with that, almost thirty-five years since Glenn's last professional game and twenty years since his death, Major League Baseball had come a long way in redeeming itself. It's an appropriate time to now ask what Glenn's legacy should be and what he would have thought about baseball's brave new world of acceptance.

As for Glenn's legacy, it's safe to surmise that he helped pave the way for future gays to come out in baseball. It's been said that the first one through any of society's so-called "walls" gets bloodied, and Glenn was no different, paying the price with his playing career. Baseball people will tell you they never saw him as a .237 lifetime hitter, but instead a five-tool player denied a fair opportunity to reach his superstar potential because of who he was.

Perhaps someday people will read this book and wonder what all the fuss was over Glenn Burke. They'll ask themselves why the Dodgers would move a popular player with as much raw, natural talent as Glenn simply because of his lifestyle. Or why the A's, the worst team in baseball when they demoted Glenn to the minor leagues, would be so concerned about Glenn being a disruptive force because of his homosexuality when he could have helped them win some games.

There is no better example of the human capacity to evolve and change personal views than when Jackie Robinson broke baseball's color barrier in 1947. How utterly ridiculous it now seems that a ballplayer previous to 1947 was denied the chance to play major-league baseball strictly based on the color of his skin.

Perhaps Glenn's legacy could best be described as that of "the gay baseball player's Jackie Robinson." The young Glenn, who used to sleep in his baseball uniform before his mother would regularly have to peel it off of him, has helped make it possible for other little boys like him to have the chance to live out their dreams.

As for what Glenn would have likely thought about the latest societal developments, and those in baseball in particular, I am sure he would have been delighted if not a bit shocked. As a man who strove to be true to himself, he sought most of his life to extinguish the stigma of one's own sexual orientation. But for all the anguish and disappointment of a baseball career and, ultimately, a life cut short, somewhere Glenn is likely very proud that, in the end, positive change was made.

His life had great meaning.

MAJOR LEAGUE BASEBALL'S PRESS CONFERENCE ON INCLUSION, JULY 15, 2014

THE MODERATOR: Good afternoon. Welcome to Fanfest. Welcome to a very special day for Major League Baseball. Very shortly we will be making a major announcement, the theme of which is inclusion. Once those involved in that announcement join the stage we will get that under way.

Hello. I'd like to welcome everyone to a very special day here at Major League Baseball. Today with me on the stage are Commissioner Selig, six-year major leaguer Billy Bean, and Lutha Burke, the older sister of the late major leaguer Glenn Burke.

We'll be making two announcements today, and the two are linked by the concept of inclusion. Over the last several years, Major League Baseball has set the goal of being more inclusive and taking important, concrete steps to achieve that very important goal.

In 2011 Major League Baseball and its players added non-discrimination protection based on sexual orientation to its collective bargaining agreement. This was a meaningful and important step in professional sports.

Last year MLB and the MLBPA collaborated once again, this time with the State of New York, to ensure protection for current and future players from discrimination and harassment based on sexual orientation.

Every player in the major and minor leagues is now subject to a workplace code of conduct that's formally aimed to promote equality and inclusion. The attorney general of New York state, Eric Schneiderman, said of Baseball's efforts: "By making a clear stand against discrimination in our workplace, our national pastime is showing national leadership in the fight to promote equal justice for all."

Today marks yet another significant step, and I would like to bring up the Commissioner of Baseball, Commissioner Bud Selig, for an important announcement.

[Applause.]

COMMISSIONER SELIG: Thank you very much. I am honored that Billy Bean and Lutha Burke have been with us for our All-Star festivities.

All-Star week is a celebration of our sport. Because of the presence of Lutha and Billy, today is a day for us to celebrate in a very meaningful way. Lutha, I am so delighted that you are here. Your brother was a pioneer. We remember him to this day and we want to tell his story.

We want the people who make a living in our game to be who they wish to be. As an institution, we will do all we can to support them.

In that spirit, we are proud to announce our hiring of former major leaguer Billy Bean as a consultant who will serve as Major League Baseball's first Ambassador of Inclusion.

[Applause.]

COMMISSIONER SELIG: Billy is going to work with us on a wide range of issues in an effort to educate major league and minor league players and many other constituents within our game. He will be a resource for our players beyond at our rookie career development program, at the winter meetings and other industry events.

Billy will play a key role in advising our office in not only gay and lesbian efforts, but on all aspects of being inclusive.

As Jeremy noted, today marks another important step for us. I am proud of our industry's united stance, but the reality, not just in baseball, but in all of our society, is that we can never do enough to ensure respect and inclusion for everyone.

Diversity is a hallmark of our sport, which is fortunate to have an inherent ability to bring people together. The people of our sport have a responsibility to act with a kind of respect and sensitivity that our game's diverse players, employees, and fans deserve.

Our staff has truly enjoyed getting to know Billy over the past few months. He has many friends in the game today, including many people that he played with. We've had constructive conversations about building inclusive environments.

I wish that our game had someone in place to whom Billy and Glenn could have turned when they played; a friend, listener, a source of support. That's why I am so delighted to make this announcement today.

Our game is more than just a national pastime. We are a social institution. No individual better exemplifies that stature than the great pioneer who changed our game and our society, Jackie Robinson, a symbol of tolerance and the power of one guy. Jackie Robinson just wanted a number on his back.

This is a game of equal opportunity for all, and I believe Billy will help us preserve that. I think it is wonderful that members of our game will turn to Billy and I know he will be an eager listener and someone who can help us in numerous ways.

Lutha, we are pleased to honor the memory of your brother. And Billy, you are a valued member of the baseball family and I am honored in welcoming you back to Major League Baseball in this very significant new capacity. Welcome to both of you.

[Applause.]

BILLY BEAN: Thank you, Commissioner Selig. I am very humbled and honored to be here today.

As a young player I was trying to play with a very difficult secret, and I was living a life of deception and secrecy from my family, my friends, the people that loved me, and the people I loved the most, as well as my teammates.

And at the time, after ten years of playing in the league, I felt the best decision was to quit and walk away than to reach out, ask someone for a little guidance, a little help, or even talk to my own family. And it wasn't much long after that, after I had walked away, that I realized how much I loved baseball and what a terrible mistake that felt like. And for the past fifteen years of my life, I have been dedicated to try to make sure that no young athlete has made that same mistake. Because once you are unable to play, you realize what a gift it is, what an honor it is.

And today I'm very proud that MLB is recognizing the social responsibility and the importance of this decision to provide and ensure an equitable and inclusive workplace. And I want to make sure that everybody understands that the history, the integrity of baseball is never going to change.

Today is about getting our young players a chance to understand their responsibility as role models that this league gives them. They are thrust into a big, shiny, wonderful world as young men, and a lot of them have not been exposed to the same things that all of us outside of the game have been.

And that's the responsibility that I am going to take very seriously. It's not here to change the way people think, ask you to be friends with someone that you're not friends with; it's just to give everyone who is a part of the MLB family a chance to be the very best they can be.

I didn't give anybody that chance. I didn't feel like there was a resource out there for me, and that is going to change for every player, for every coach, umpire, manager, every stakeholder. Everyone involved in something like this, they're going to know that they have a place to go if they choose to go there. Someone to talk to.

And for me to be asked to come back by the Commissioner's office to be a part of baseball, it a tremendous honor and one I take very seriously. And I love baseball. I am a baseball player. I walked away, I have been away for a long time. But if you ask anyone who ever played, that never changes.

Last night the Commissioner was very gracious enough to invite me up to his suite to watch a little bit of the Home Run Derby and meet some people, and I got a chance to meet Hank Aaron. And I was thinking to myself, Hank Aaron was asked to be a role model in a very difficult time in the civil rights movement. He may have never expected that to be part of his life. But because he is a great baseball player, people looked up to him. What he said mattered.

And these young players, our veterans, our young ones, minor leaguers, we are going to give them a chance to understand that what they say and what they do matters to the fans all around this country, especially in today's day and age with social media, every word, every action is documented. And I've learned firsthand what it means when someone says something negative, maybe as a joke, something sexist, something that was not meant for anyone else to hear, that it is damaging to someone when they look up to that person.

So today I just think that baseball is proving their history will remain intact and they are going to continue to lead instead of follow and watch by the sidelines.

It is a tremendous honor for me to be here, and I thank the Commissioner very, very much for allowing me this opportunity.

[Applause.]

THE MODERATOR: On behalf of everyone, Billy, welcome back to baseball.

Another member of the deep and rich baseball family is a player named Glenn Burke. He played for the Dodgers and the A's from 1976 to 1979. At that time only Glenn's team knew that he was gay. Unfortunately, Glenn died of complications from AIDS in 1985 and Billy wrote his book entitled *Going the Other Way* in Glenn's memory.

We are very honored that the pioneer that was Glenn Burke, his sister, Lutha Burke, has joined us here today. And Lutha, I would like to invite you to say a few remarks.

[Applause.]

LUTHA BURKE: Hello. I am usually used to being in the background, not the forefront. But there are a couple of things that I would like to say.

I would like to thank the MLB for honoring my brother in such a fashion, that makes my family and myself very proud. And I would like to thank Glenn's family and his friends and his fans, or his fans and his friends, because Glenn considered his fans his friends and his friends his fans.

I have no doubt that Glenn would be very happy today and would probably wonder why all the folderol, because when you are just busy trying to live a life and be a decent human being, and play the sport as best you can, with all the respect you can, it should be a done deal or an easy deal. And for that I would like to thank you very much and thank MLB for having myself and my daughter, to honor or stand in for him. Thank you.

[Applause.]

THE MODERATOR: Thank you so much, Lutha, and thank you, Billy, and thank you to the Commissioner. A big round of applause for this historic moment in Major League Baseball.

[Applause.]

THE MODERATOR: Thank you so much for your attention, ladies and gentlemen, as we continue with our announcements today. Again, so significant and so important, the next portion of today's program addresses a different partnership that Major League Baseball has been working on and forging over the last year.

For his remarks on that new partnership, MLB Chief Operating Officer, Rob Manfred.

[Applause.]

ROB MANFRED: Good afternoon. For the last year or so we have been working extensively with a not-for-profit group, Athlete Ally. The purpose of Athlete Ally is to end homophobia and transphobia in sports.

Over the past year Athlete Ally has been very active in our space. They were present at the winter meetings in Orlando, they were involved in the rookie career development program that was held last January. They participated in the diversity summit that Wendy Lewis, who is here with us today, coordinated in New York in May.

And today we would like to announce the next step in our relationship with Athlete Ally. We are forming a strategic alliance, the purpose of which is to provide education and training on respect and inclusion in our workplace. Athlete Ally will work not only with players, but also with front office personnel on these issues.

Major League Baseball and Commissioner Selig are extremely proud of the efforts that we have made in the area of inclusion. The announcement welcoming Billy Bean back to Major League Baseball as our Ambassador for Inclusion is an important one.

In addition, we have been working with various groups involved in the LGBT community to develop an internship program. We'll have an intern at 245 Park in the Commissioner's office, as well as at MLB.com. I'd like to especially thank Bob Bowman, the CEO of MLB.com, for his support of this effort. I'd also like to thank Hudson Taylor for his assistance in identifying qualified candidates.

As Commissioner Selig said earlier, it is very important to all of us that the national pastime remain a symbol of inclusiveness as we move forward. Thank you very much.

[Applause.]

THE MODERATOR: Thanks so much, Rob. And as the day presses on, as this new partnership strives forward, let me introduce you to the founder of Athlete Ally, Hudson Taylor. Hudson, come on up.

[Applause.]

HUDSON TAYLOR: I want to start by thanking Rob Manfred, Commissioner Selig, and all of Major League Baseball for their continued commitment to creating a welcoming workplace and fan environment, regardless of sexual orientation or gender identity.

The principles of respect and inclusion have always been central to the identity of baseball. And Athlete Ally is honored to partner with the league on continuing this legacy.

Over the last year Athlete Ally has had the privilege of working with players and personnel on respect and inclusion. We have been inspired by these conversations and interactions and look forward to continuing this strategic alliance so every athlete, employee, and fan knows that MLB's commitment to the LBGT community is second to none.

Creating inclusive cultures requires explicitly inclusive actions. Today's honoring of Glenn Burke's legacy and of his family, the league's hiring of Billy Bean, its announcement of LGBT internships, and this strategic alliance with Athlete Ally shows baseball is committed to creating an inclusive culture.

Thank you, Rob, and Commissioner Selig, for your continued leadership. Thank you, Glenn Burke and your family, and

Billy Bean, and really, every LBGT athlete, every LBGT coach and fan for bringing this issue to the forefront by sharing your experience with the world.

And lastly, thank you Major League Baseball, for inviting Athlete Ally to join you on this journey to making the sport of baseball welcoming for all. Thank you so much.

[Applause.]

THE MODERATOR: Ladies and gentlemen, that concludes this historic day. Thank you, Rob, thank you, Hudson. Enjoy the rest of your day.

ACKNOWLEDGMENTS

The authors of this book would like to thank Rob Wilson, literary agent, the Baseball Hall of Fame and Museum, Pamela Pitts and the Oakland A's organization, and GMHC for their assistance in making this project a reality. Sincere gratitude also goes to the team at the Berkley Publishing Group, with special thanks to editor Denise Silvestro and assistant editor Allison Janice.

Glenn Burke, a former center fielder for the Los Angeles Dodgers and the Oakland Athletics, over a span of five seasons, appeared in the 1977 World Series and is widely recognized as the person to have invented the high five. Burke made history with his 1982 public admission of being the first major league baseball player to reveal his homosexuality. He died of AIDS-related complications in 1995.

Erik Sherman is the bestselling coauthor of *Steve Blass: A Pirate for Life* and *Mookie: Life, Baseball and the '86 Mets*, which made the *New York Times* sports hardcover bestseller list in 2014. His work has appeared in the *Pittsburgh Post-Gazette* and the *Bergen Record*. He has contributed to baseball documentaries produced by ESPN, Comcast SportsNet, and Root Sports, and his speaking engagements have taken him from the National Baseball Hall of Fame in Cooperstown, New York, to the Yogi Berra Museum in Montclair, New Jersey. He is a graduate of Emerson College and blogs regularly at ErikShermanBaseball.com. He currently resides in New Rochelle, New York, with his wife and two children.

Printed in the United States
by Baker & Taylor Publisher Services